THE GREAT PYRAMID DECODED

W9-AXK-145

by

E. RAYMOND CAPT M.A., A.I.A., F.S.A. Scot.

Archaeological Institute of America

PUBLISHED BY

HOFFMAN PRINTING CO.
P.O. Box 1529
Muskogee, Oklahoma 74402
(918) 682-8341
www.artisanpublishers.com

ISBN 0-934666-01-6
Library of Congress catalog card number: 78 - 101677

THE SPHINX AND PYRAMID

PREFACE

Jeremiah 32: 18-29 states that God—

"...hast set signs and wonders in the land of Egypt, even unto this day."

In Egypt are found over 80 pyramids, built over a period of 1000 years, between the 27th and 18th centuries B.C. The most famous are the Pyramids of Giza. Only three are of any note, or size, and the smaller ones are now little more than ruins. Of these three, the largest is the Great Pyramid.

Who has not wondered about the Great Pyramid of Giza? It has always ranked first among the pyramids of Egypt and is the only remaining one of the Seven Wonders of the Ancient World. Thus it proves itself to be the greatest and most enduring of all.

What story does it tell? The monuments of Egypt are covered with hieroglyphic writing. Their record may be easily read by the expert. The Great Pyramid in this respect is silent. If it has a message, that message is not on the surface for anyone to read—and forget.

In our day, Pyramidology, with the aids of modern archaeology and scientific research, has unlocked the secret of the Pyramid of Giza. The Great Pyramid stands decoded. It is the greatest archaeological discovery of all times. The evidence of this has been collected for us. There is no need for imagination or assumption. Let us analyze the evidence and translate it into as simple English as the technical nature of the subject matter will permit.

THE GREAT PYRAMID FROM THE AIR
(looking south-east)

HISTORICAL RECORD

Although the Pharoah in whose reign the Great Pyramid was built, was Khufu (Cheops), second king of the Fourth Egyptian Dynasty, all the evidence supports the record of Herodotus that "strangers to Egypt" supervised the building of the Great Pyramid.

Herodotus, who has been called "The Father of History," wrote that Cheops reigned 50 years, and that his brother Cephren, who succeeded to the kingdom, reigned 56 years. Thus, he adds, "106 years are reckoned, during which the Egyptians suffered all kinds of calamities; and for this length of time the temples were closed and never opened."

Manetho, an Egyptian priest, explains that the temples were closed during the time of the Shepherd Kings (Cory's Ancient Fragments, pg. 68). He writes, "...there came up from the East, in a strange manner, men of an ignoble race, who had the confidence to invade our country, and easily subdued it by their power, without a battle. All this nation," continues Manetho, "was styled Hycsos, the Shepherd Kings. The first syllable, 'Hyc', according to the sacred dialect denoted a king, and the 'sos' signifies a shepherd according to the vulgar tongue; and of these is compounded the term Hycsos. Some say they were Arabians."

Archbishop Ussher, the noted Church historian, in his chronology, refers to the migration of the Shepherd Kings from Arabia into Egypt. From Ussher and other authorities, it seems that some "Shepherd-Prince" coming from Arabia or Palestine was enabled to exert such an amount of mental control over King Cheops as to induce the King to shut up the idolatrous temples and compel his subjects to labour in the erection of the Great Pyramid. Under this "shepherd-prince," Egypt's national religion was overturned in favour of the more simple worship of the One God.

Upon completion of the Great Pyramid, ancient writings of the historians say that the "foreign" people withdrew and their departure was the cause of great rejoicing among the Egyptians. The restraint being removed, the people returned with fresh zest to their idolatrous practices.

Bible chronology and findings of archaeology have established the date of the start of the building of the Great Pyramid at 2623 B.C. This has caused many Egyptologists to dispute today the Hyksos theory since modern archaeologists have labeled a much later migration into Egypt as Hyksos, and assigned a period (1800-1500 B.C.) as their domination of parts of Egypt.

It is generally agreed, however, that the beginnings of Hyksos control of Egypt are obscure and that during the period of the Third and Fourth Dynasties the Egyptians furnished the labor for the erection of several pyramids, culminating in the Great Pyramid.

Herodotus informs us that the construction of the Great Pyramid commenced only when a sufficient force of skilled masons was available. He wrote, "They worked to the number of one hundred thousand men at a time, each party three months." It took 20 years labor although some records add 10 years for cutting stone and preparing the site.

According to Professor Flinders Petrie, one three month period fell during the inundation of the Nile, when field-work was at a stand-still and the services of 100,000 men for transporting the stones could be easily obtained. The stone-cutters and masons were probably engaged all the year round in the quarries and on the pyramid itself.

Herodotus continues: "This pyramid was first built in the form of a flight of steps. After the workmen had completed the pyramid in this form, (probably by means of four ramps, one on each side increasing in height around the pyramid as the pyramid heightened - author) they raised other stones (casing stones) by means of machines, made of short beams, from the ground of the first tier of steps; and after the stone was placed there it was raised to the second tier by another machine; for there were as many machines as there was tiers of steps; or perhaps the same machine, if it was easily moved was raised from one tier to the other, as it was required for lifting the stones."

Herodotus also states that Cheops never used the Great Pyramid as a tomb, but was buried elsewhere, namely "in a subterranean region on a island there surrounded by the waters of the Nile." This is confirmed by the historian Diodorus Siculus who says Cheops was buried "in an abscure place." An additional archaeological confirmation has recently been discovered in an inscription on a scarab found by the Egyptologist Abdul Moneim Abu Bakr which speaks of the "Southern Tomb of Khufu." The Southern Tomb is obviously not a pyramid, which would not conform to Diodorus' description "an obscure place."

Both the second and third Pyramids were clearly intended to serve as sepulchres for the kings who built them, and it has been erroneously concluded, by some, that the Great Pyramid was built for the same purpose.

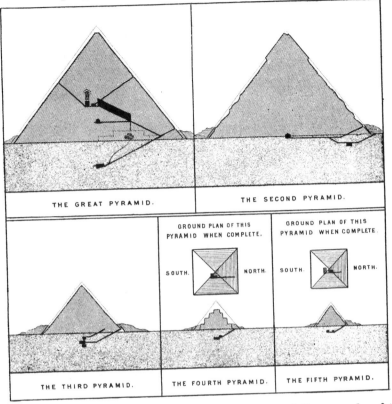

THE GREAT PYRAMID.

THE SECOND PYRAMID.

GROUND PLAN OF THIS PYRAMID WHEN COMPLETE.

GROUND PLAN OF THIS PYRAMID WHEN COMPLETE.

SOUTH. NORTH.

SOUTH. NORTH.

THE THIRD PYRAMID.

THE FOURTH PYRAMID.

THE FIFTH PYRAMID.

In historical times many well-known visitors left records of their descriptions of the Great Pyramid, but perhaps the first modern traveler who carefully and successfully examined the Pyramid was Nicholas Shaw in 1721. He was soon followed by others including John Greaves, Professor of Astronomy at Oxford University. Greaves began the first truly scientific study and investigation of the Great Pyramid, thoroughly exploring the structure. In 1737 he published his "Pyramidographia" giving the results of his laborious observations and measurements.

In 1798, the French defeated the Ottoman Turks at the "Battle of the Pyramids" and Napoleon became master of Egypt. At this time, the engineers of Napoleon's army explored the Pyramid. While making measurements they uncovered much valuable information.

7

It was they who discovered the corner sockets, peculiar to no other pyramid, and also the relationship of the Pyramid's structure and dimensions to astronomical science.

In 1817, Caviglia, a bold, but illiterate and fanciful seaman, became intrigued by the mystery of the Great Pyramid. He became convinced that there were still undiscovered passages in the interior of the Pyramid. Giving up the sea he settled down to explore the Pyramid and other neighboring monuments. Although Caviglia never found any "secret" passages, his efforts in cleaning out the known passage system elicited new facts regarding the interior of the Pyramid.

Colonel Howard Vyse, in 1830, was the next to make significant progress in lifting the veil of mystery from the Great Pyramid. With the help of a hundred hired laborors, he cleaned the passages of the Pyramid, then made measurements and observations. Colonel Vyse succeeded in interesting Sir John Hershal, the great English astronomer, who became convinced that the Pyramid, in its design and construction, evidenced a wonderful knowledge of astronomy, applied mathematics and other scientific information, predating our recorded knowledge by several thousand years.

Mr. Robert Menzies, of Leith, Scotland, is given credit for being the first to attract general attention to the assertion that the Great Pyramid was a treasury of Divinely given wisdom embodying chronological, meteorological, astronomical, mathematical, historical and Biblical truth. He also contended that this storehouse of wisdom remained sealed by Divine appointment, to be revealed to those now living; to whom these truths would bear witness, at a time when they would be most needed.

Later, John Taylor, a London publisher, gifted mathematician and amateur astronomer, began a study of the measurements of the Pyramid in order to analyze the results from a mathematician's point of view. His conclusion was that the architect of the Great Pyramid was not an Egyptian, either by race or religion. He believed it would be found, eventually, that the measurements and contours of the structures' passage system, and its chambers, were intended to indicate and symbolize a prophetic and historical record, especially in relationship to Biblical revelation.

It remained, however, for Professor Piazzi Smyth, Astronomer for Scotland, to lift investigation and study of the Pyramid into the realm of applied science. With his wife, this astronomer spent many months at the Great Pyramid, directing a large group of assistants who made scientifically accurate measurements and observations. The results were published, in three large volumes, nearly a century ago.

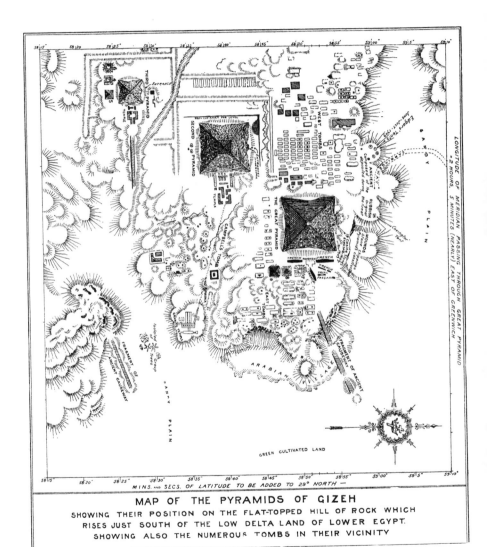

MAP OF THE PYRAMIDS OF GIZEH
SHOWING THEIR POSITION ON THE FLAT-TOPPED HILL OF ROCK WHICH RISES JUST SOUTH OF THE LOW DELTA LAND OF LOWER EGYPT. SHOWING ALSO THE NUMEROUS TOMBS IN THEIR VICINITY

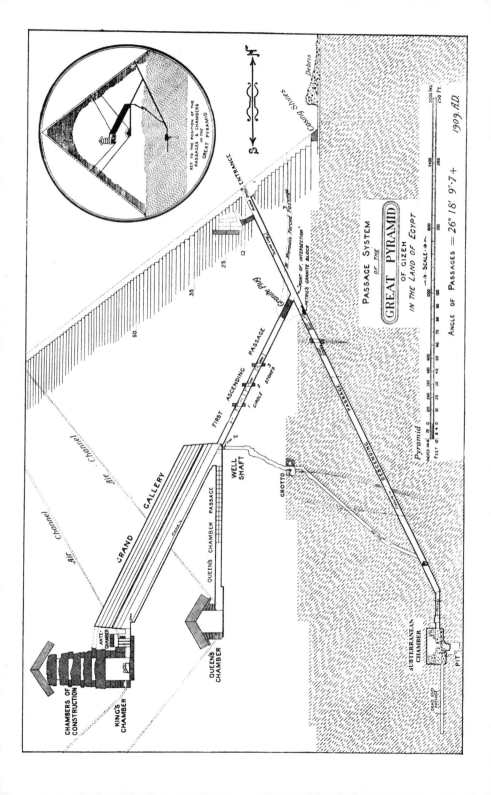

PASSAGE SYSTEM
of the
GREAT PYRAMID
OF GIZEH
IN THE LAND OF EGYPT

Angle of Passages = 26° 18' 9"·7 +

1909 A.D.

GEOGRAPHICAL LOCATION

Situated ten miles to the southwest of Cairo, the capital of Egypt, the Great Pyramid stands on the northern edge of the Giza (Gizeh) Plateau, 198 feet above sea level, in the eastern extremity of the Libyan section of the Great Sahara Desert.

The Great Pyramid was placed in the exact center of all the land area of the world. Lines drawn through the north-south and east-west axis of the Pyramid divide equally the earth's terrain. The north-south axis (31° 9' meridian east of Greenwich) is the longest land meridian, and the east-west axis (29°58' 51' north), the longest land parallel.

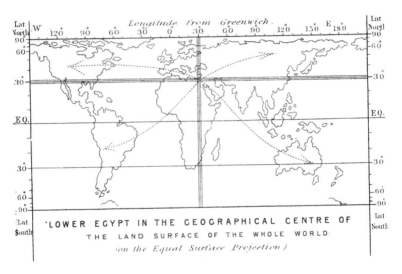

'LOWER EGYPT IN THE GEOGRAPHICAL CENTRE OF THE LAND SURFACE OF THE WHOLE WORLD: (on the Equal Surface Projection)

That the Architect knew where to find the poles of the earth is evidenced by the high degree of accuracy in orienting the building true north. Modern man's best effort, the Paris Observatory, is six minutes of a degree off true north. The Great Pyramid today is only off three minutes and that after 4200 years, due mainly to subsidence.

Such near perfect orientation is exceedingly hard to secure, even with modern astronomical equipment, and seemingly impossible without it. If the knowledge of the magnetic needle was known it would have been of little value. It points to the magnetic north, not to the true north. The celestial pole is a point, usually a star, through which the polar axis of the earth would pass were it projected to the star sphere.

11

Lines produced from the two diagonals of the Pyramid, to the northwest and northeast, enclose the Nile Delta; thus embracing the fan-shaped country of Lower Egypt.

THE NILE-DELTA QUADRANT

The Great Pyramid of Gizeh stands at the geometric center and yet at the southern extremity of the Quadrant

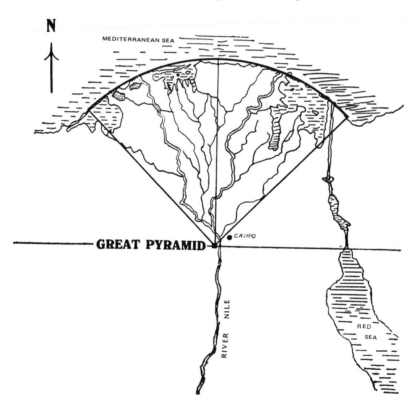

The southern extremity, being the northernmost edge of the Giza plateau where the Great Pyramid stands looking over the fan-shaped sector of Egypt, was in ancient times at the boundary where the cultivated land touched the desert. This plateau was called Giza, which is the Arabic word for edge or border. It was this unusual location that first suggested the Great Pyramid was the monument spoken of in the Scriptures by Isaiah the prophet:

Isaiah 19: 19-20

"In that day shall there be an altar to the Lord in the midst of the land of Egypt, and a pillar (Hebrew "Matstsebah" correctly translated means monument) *at the border thereof to the Lord. And it shall be for a sign, and for a witness unto the Lord of Hosts in the land of Egypt."*

Since the full official name of the Pyramid, the Great Pyramid of Giza, means, in English, the Great Pyramid of the Border, the answer to the apparently contradictory definition of Isaiah is found in the Great Pyramid. The only spot on the face of the earth that completely answers this description, both geometrically and geographically, is the precise place where the Great Pyramid actually stands.

Map showing position of the Great Pyramid

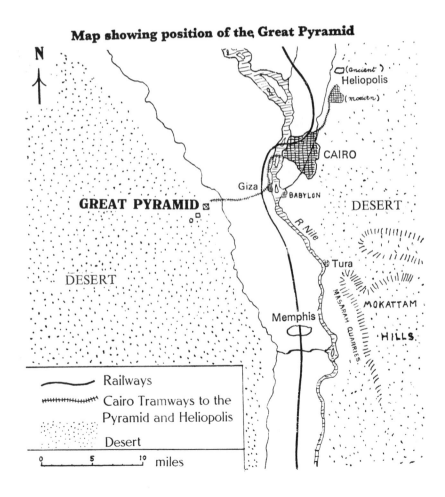

13

NEAR VIEW OF THE GREAT PYRAMID FROM THE AIR

PHYSICAL APPEARANCE

The Great Pyramid is the largest building in the world and covers slightly over 13 acres. It contains nearly 90,000,000 cubic feet of masonry, enough to build 30 Empire State buildings.

With the exception of the comparatively small space occupied by the passages and chambers, the Great Pyramid is a solid mass of masonry having a huge square base and four tapering sides that rise to a small platform at the apex. The corners of the base are marked by socket stones sunk into the solid rock.

The original side length is 755 ¾ feet and the height up to the top, as the builders left it unfinished, is 454½ feet. The height as planned by the builders and as evidenced from the Architect's original design is 485 feet, equal to a 48-story modern skyscraper.

The top piece, or capstone, was never set, having been rejected by the builders. It should be pointed out that the capstone (Head Stone) is also the chief cornerstone, since all the four corners of the building converge in that one stone at the top. Thus it alone, of all the stones in the structure, is the only one that is over all the four corners.

In its original state, shining in the sun, and so reflecting its rays, the Great Pyramid was supposed to be visible from the moon as a brilliant star on earth. This phenomenon was caused by the smooth highly polished limestone blocks of which the Pyramid was originally covered. These blocks, called casing stones, covered the four sides. Each side having an area of five and one quarter acres, acted as gigantic mirrors, reflecting great beams of light that could be seen for many miles around.

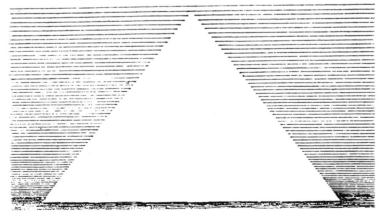

By means of its reflections and shadows, the Great Pyramid became the great sundial of Egypt, not only for the days and hours, but for the seasons of the year. Exactly as a modern chronometer gives the hours, say of midnight, 6 a.m., noon, and 6 p.m., so the reflections from the Pyramid gave accurately the days upon which the Winter Solstice, the Spring Equinox, the Summer Solstice, and the Autumnal Equinox occurred. This precisely defined the Solar Astronomical Year.

Noon of the Summer Solstice was the point when the Great Pyramid's triangular reflections were most notable and the Pyramid cast no shadows. These are respectively the shortest noon reflections of the year from the South, East, and West faces of the Pyramid, and the longest noon reflection of the year from the North face of the Pyramid.

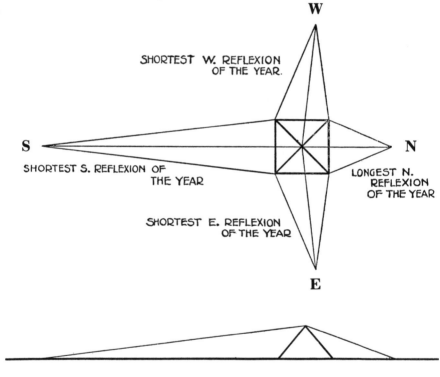

By contrast, at noon on the Winter Solstice, the Great Pyramid's northern face, in which is the Entrance, was in the shade and a shadow was cast on the ground (at the north side) while the sun-light on the south side was reflected back into the air.

The solid beams of reflected light proceeding from the East and West face slopes of the Pyramid at noon had a further remarkable property defining Winter as distinct from Spring, Summer, and Autumn. The East and West noon reflected beams each had a surface seen from the North side of the Pyramid, and a surface seen from the South side of the Pyramid. These noon reflected beams each had a sharply defined ridge running from the Pyramid apex to the apex of each of the images projected on the ground, and as viewed from the South, always, throughout the year, appeared inclining away from the observer. The side of the East or West noon reflected beam, however, as viewed from the North side of the Pyramid, appeared inclining away from the observer during Spring, Summer, and Autumn, but appeared overhanging towards the observer during Winter as shown on the following diagram.

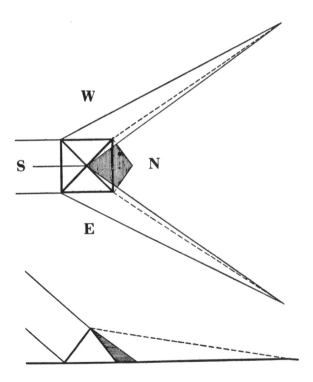

The great earthquake of the 13th century C.E. shook the structure, cracked its face and dislodged some of the casing stones. These loose stones gave an idea to builders in the nearby cities. They began to use the Pyramid as a quarry, with the result that in a few centuries all but a few casing stones, hidden by sand, were stripped from the face, leaving the core masonry as we see it today, exposed to erosion by the elements.

The core masonry is composed largely of coarse limestone (nummulitic), mostly from the Giza Plateau itself, on which the Pyramid is built. The number of these yellow limestone blocks was estimated at about 2,300,000 by Sir Flinders Petrie, Egyptologist. They average approximately two and one half tons each, but many are considerably heavier.

The few casing stones found "in situ" by Colonel Howard Vyse, Egyptologist, in 1837, made it possible to determine the original baseline of the structure and also the exact angle of its sloping sides.

The casing stones consist of dense, white, marble-like limestone and exhibit an amount of accuracy in fitting that equals the most modern optician's work. The joints, with an area of some 35 square feet each, are not thicker than aluminum foil; yet they include, between the polished surfaces, an extraordinarily thin film of white cement.

Colonel H. Vyse, speaking of the the cement says, "...such is the tenacity of this cement...that a fragment of a stone that has been destroyed remains firmly fixed in its original alignment, notwithstanding the lapse of time and the violence to which it has been exposed." Modern chemists have analyzed this cement but have been unable to compound one of such fineness and tenacity as that exhibited in the Great Pyramid.

Petrie in his account of these stones records, "The mean thickness of the joints is one-fiftieth part of an inch; and the mean variation of the cutting of the stone from a straight line, and from the true square, is but one-hundredth part of an inch in the length of 75 inches up the face." That they were able to maintain these tolerances despite the area and the weight of the stone to be moved—some 16 to 20 tons each—is seemingly almost impossible. This feat was duplicated in all the casing stones, which were estimated to have numbered approximately 144,000.

Today, the Pyramid, at a distance, looks like a great rock pile. Nearer at hand, it is seen that the stones, composing the structure, which are roughly cut, are laid in even courses, one upon another. These courses form a series of gigantic steps, sloping back from the base on all four sides, to a level platform at the top.

TRANSPORTING THE STONE

How the ancient Egyptians moved the stone from the quarries to the Pyramid being built has been the subject of much speculation. As we know, the Great Pyramid used millions of tons of stone, most of which were in 2½ ton blocks. This was no easy undertaking, yet the Egyptians managed to accomplish this task.

If we look at a map of ancient Egypt we will see how they did it. The Great Pyramid, as well as all of the other pyramids, lie near the Nile River. Most of the stone quarries of Egypt are also located near and up the river from the pyramids. The obvious solution was to carry the stone in boats down the Nile.

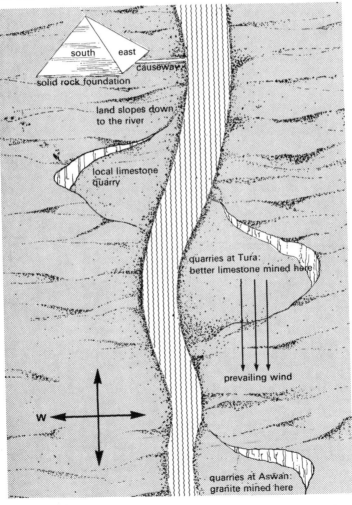

Several quarry sites have been, by petrological identification, found to be the source of the stone used in the construction of the Great Pyramid. One site, near the Great Pyramid provided a poorer-quality limestone; Tura, a site farther up the Nile produced a better limestone; and the red (pink) granite came from the Aswan quarries even farther up the Nile.

The most logical type of boat used to convey the stone down the Nile was the large flat-bottomed barges, illustrations of which are found on wall sculptures and paintings. Rowers on each side provided the main means of moving the boats, but to take advantage of any wind which might arise, a large square sail was attached to a single mast in the center of the boat. At the rear of the boat was a large paddle-shaped rudder which the helmsmen used to steer the boat.

NILE BOAT

To get the stones from the quarries to the river which was in some cases nearly a mile away, sledges were used. The stones were first levered onto the sledge, probably from a ledge or ramp above it, then tied firmly on with ropes. Ropes were then attached to the front of the sledge and held by a gang of men who pulled the sledge. Water or some other liquid was poured on the ground to help the sledge slide along. In areas where sand had to be traversed, a bed of logs could have been laid and rollers placed under the sledge as it was pulled, using the house-mover's technique of continually taking the rollers from back to front as they came out from under the sledge.

The number of men needed to pull the sledge depended on the number and weight of the stones it carried, and as labour was plentiful this was no problem to the Egyptians. Using a tested ratio of 16 men to a ton, most of the core masonry (average 2-1/2 tons each) would have needed less than 50 men pulling over hard ground; using the roller technique, the number of pullers could be reduced considerably.

Moving the stone from the boats to the Pyramid site would have been a more difficult task because unlike the quarries usually above the river banks (allowing gravity to assist in the pulling of the sledges) the pyramids were uphill from the river docking sites. However, each pyramid had a causeway connecting it to the Nile. This was just a road cut out of the rock with walls on either side and a roof, except for the two earliest which did not have a roof. The causeways were intended to serve eventually as a road for the funeral procession when it traveled from the river to the pyramid. It would be built at the same time that the pyramid site was being prepared. Prior to the causeway being roofed over, it could be used as a road for the sledges bringing the stone from the boats to the building site.

Such a causeway or road to the Great Pyramid from the Nile River is still traceable. It terminated on the East side of the Pyramid. Herodotus states that before the Pyramid building was begun they spent ten years in preparing the site, during which time they constructed a road "for the transport of the stones from the Nile...the length of the road amounts to five stadia (1017 yds.), its breadth is ten fathoms (60 ft.), and its height, at the highest places, is eight fathoms (48 ft.), and it is constructed entirely of polished stone with figures engraved on it."

THE FIVE SOCKETS OF THE GREAT PYRAMID

AT THE BASE

showing their relative positions

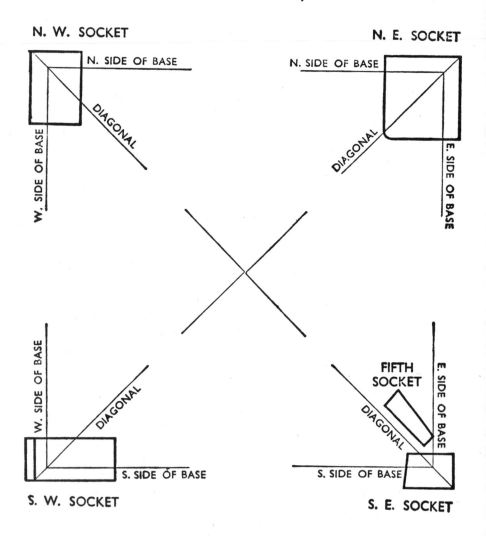

THE CORNER SOCKETS

An amazing, scientifically engineered feature of the Great Pyramid, distinguishing it from all the other pyramids, is found in the wonderfully devised corner-sockets. All who know anything of modern engineering are aware of the ingenious devices by which shocks, stresses and strains caused by expansion and contraction of the materials of which the structures are composed are compensated for. These devices consist of roller-bearings, expansion joints, or ball and socket arrangements which care for these stresses and strains without communicating them to the main structure.

Excavators, removing the debris about the base of the Great Pyramid, found mortises, some eight by fifteen feet in size, cut into the natural rock, at each of the four corners. Into these mortises were placed heavy, carefully chiseled rocks, anchoring the four sloping corner-edges of the structure. These anchorage-blocks were so placed as to allow a space between the sides of the mortises and the corner stones, thus allowing expansion caused by changes of temperature or earthquakes, serving the purpose of ball and socket joints.

S.E. SOCKET OF THE GREAT PYRAMID
with the 5th socket in the background

These corner-sockets and casing-stones, still remaining in place, make possible the reconstruction of the Pyramid as originally completed. This reconstruction of design is absolutely essential in restoring original dimensions and measurements upon which the interpretation of the Great Pyramid's passage-system is based. However, difficult this may seem to the reader, these details are easily determined by skilled engineer or architect, having these few stones remaining in place, from which to determine exact measurements and angles.

These socket-bedded corner-stones demonstrate that over four thousand years ago the builders of the Great Pyramid understood the workings of natural laws and also knew how to allow for their effects. They also give evidence of the foresight and engineering skill on the part of the Pyramid's Architect, which characterizes every detail of the edifice, and awaken the admiration and wonder of all engineers and scientists who have visited the structure.

N.E. SOCKET OF THE GREAT PYRAMID

PYRAMID OPENED

No record has been found to indicate the interior of the Great Pyramid was penetrated before A.D. 820, when Caliph Al Maanoun of Bagdad came to Egypt to seek the hidden wealth reportedly hidden within its secret recesses. He supposed this largest and finest of all the pyramids to contain fabulous treasure beyond description.

Al Mamoun determined to force the building of the Great Pyramid to disclose its secrets, and so he directed his Mohommedan workman to begin to excavate near the base of the middle of the northern side. With the crude implements which the time afforded they laboriously forced a tunnel about 40 yards into the structure, not knowing the real entrance was about 25 feet away to the east.

But one day, when the exhausted workers were about to quit in despair, they hear a dull thud of a stone falling in some hollow space; within no more than a few feet on one side of them. Energetically, they started digging anew, in the direction of the strange noise. Hammering away they finally burst into the descending passage.

Here was exposed what had been hidden from the Egyptians for centuries; for the falling of that stone revealed the chief leading secret of the building. The large angular fitting stone fitted into the ceiling of the inclined and narrow passage quite undistinguishable from the other part of the ceiling, had now dropped on to the floor before their eyes. Revealed in the space from where the stone had fallen was the beginning of another passage, clearly ascending upward from the descending passage. However, a series of huge granite plugs or square wedge-like shapes were immovably jammed in the passage.

The exuberant workers, following the open and downward sloping passage to its end, found a deep cavernous chamber approximately 100 feet vertically down in the natural rock under the Pyramid's foundation. Here to their disappointment, they found nothing but the unfinished, roughly hewn chamber containing in the floor a square cut well shaft leading nowhere. On the far side of the chamber, an even narrower horizontal passage led some 50 feet to a blank wall.

Returning some 276 feet back up the downward sloping passage, the Arabs turned their attention to the peculiar granite plug blocking the upward sloping passage. To break it in pieces within the confined entrance passage space seemed quite out of the question, it being of indeterminate length and evidently weighing several tons, so they

began cutting away the smaller ordinary masonry along the west side
of the granite.

THE GRANITE PLUG

As the Arab's chisels penetrated the softer limestone blocks they
found the granite plug was actually three plugs totalling about 15 feet
in length. Beyond the third plug they found themselves in a passage
sloping upward but again blocked. But this time the filling material
was only limestone which could be cracked with chisels and removed
piece by piece. It was a matter of time before the passage above the
granite plug was free from obstruction.

In front of them, on first entering the tall gallery, but on the
level, they saw another low, narrow (hornizontal) passage. Following
this passage they found themselves in a rectangular limestone
chamber with a rough floor and a gabled limestone roof. The room,
about 18 feet long and nearly square, had an empty nitch in the east
wall. The Arabs, thinking the nitch might conceal the entrance to
another chamber, hacked their way into its solid masonry for a few
feet before deciding there was only limestone core masonry behind.

Returning to the entrance of the horizontal passage, the Arabs examined the tall gallery-chamber. This new passage continued upward at the same slope as the preceeding passage. On each side was a narrow bench or shelf, slotted at regular intervals. At the top of the gallery they came upon a huge solid stone (level on the top) raised about three feet above the sloping floor of the gallery. Beyond this platform, the floor continued level through another low passage. A third of the way along this passage, it widened and heightened into a sort of ante-chamber, allowing Al Mamoun's men to raise their heads before again being obliged to stoop along the short passage which led to yet another chamber.

The torches of the Arabs revealed a great and well proportioned room; the walls, floor and ceiling were all of beautifully squared and polished red-granite blocks. So finely jointed were the stones that the point of a pen knife could not be made to penetrate the joints. Because of its comparable large size and flat ceiling, the Arabs named it the "King's Chamber".

To the amazement of the Arabs, there was no sign of treasure. They searched frantically but could find nothing of interest or value, only a large coffer or sarcophagus of highly polished granite, which when struck gave off a bell-like sound. In the fury of disappointment, the Arabs ripped up part of the floor and hacked at the walls in a vain attempt to find another hidden passage.

Legend has it the Caliph was astounded. His quarriers, infuriated over their deception into such enormous, unrequited and fruitless labors, began to murmur threats against him. To appease the men's rising indignation toward him, Al Mamoun commanded his discontents to go dig at a spot where he indicated.

There they soon came upon a sum of gold, exactly equal to the wages claimed for their work, which gold he had himself secretly deposited at the place. When it was found, he could not repress his astonishment that the mighty king who built the pyramid was so full of inspiration as to be able to count so truly what it cost in Arab labor to break open his pyramid.

But the great mysterious structure was now open. For centuries the Arabians, when able to overcome their superstitious fears, went in and out.

The ENTRANCE of the Great Pyramid of Gizeh

INTERIOR

The only true entrance to the Great Pyramid from the outside is located on the north side of the Pyramid 286.1 inches east of the north-south axis and at a point about fifty feet (perpendicularly) above the base-level of the structure. Its swivel stone door was constructed and hung so perfectly that it was indistinguishable from the other casing stones.

There are two systems of passages and chambers in the interior of the Great Pyramid - a downward system and an upward system. The upward system embraces two great series: (1) an ascending series made up of the Ascending Passage, Grand Gallery, King's Chamber Passage, and the King's Chamber itself; and (2) a horizontal series comprising the Queen's Chamber Passage and the Queen's Chamber. (see dia. pg. 36).

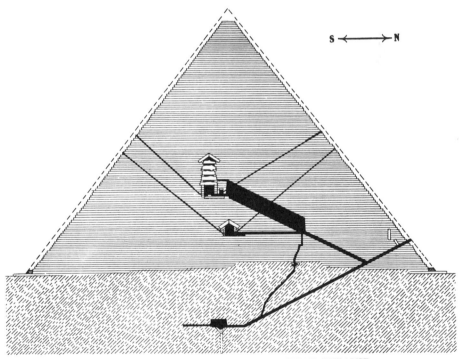

PASSAGES AND CHAMBERS IN THE GREAT PYRAMID

There is one strange, well-like passage common to both systems of passages. Starting with a torn and ragged opening from the beginning of the Grand Gallery, it bores irregularly and somewhat tortuously down through the masonry and original rock until it pierces the west wall of the Descending Passage far below the ground level. This passage, known as the Well Shaft, is thought by some scholars to have been for the purpose of making periodic inspections of the foundation for signs of weakening under the crushing weight of the pyramid.

It appears to have originally terminated in a small natural cavity known as the Grotto, some distance below the Grand Gallery, starting from a point in the west side of the Descending Passage about 86½ feet below the Pyramid's base level. At some later date, possibly after some strong and severe earthquake shocks, it was thought imperative to make a thorough examination of the upper chambers. The shaft was then forced up through the floor of the Grand Gallery.

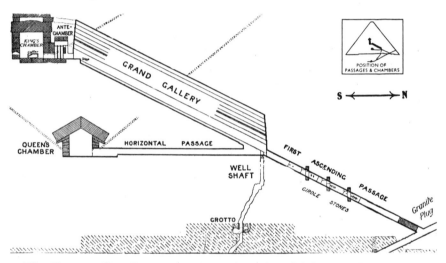

The Descending Passage, about four feet high and three and one half feet wide, originally sloped down at an angle of 26° 18' 10'. After reaching the ground level, it continues downward into natural rock and finally gains access to the great underground cavity termed the Subterranean Chamber. There is a deep vertical shaft in the bottom of this chamber known as the Bottomless Pit.

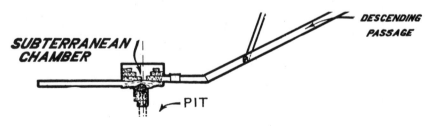

The Ascending Passage, which slopes upward at the same angle that the Descending Passage slopes downward, meets the roof of the Descending Passage vertically over a point in the floor 1170 P. (pyramid) inches from the original opening. (Pyramid inches are the units of measurement in the structural design of the Great Pyramid which will be dealt with more fully in later pages.)

The Ascending Passage however is blocked by the granite plug only 14½ inches from the entrance. This granite plug is 15 feet long and is composed of three blocks of red granite, cut square and tapered and tightly wedged in the passage, allowing no play. Therefore, it can be concluded that they were placed there during the construction of the passageway itself, before the structure reached a higher level.

Above this plug, the Ascending Passage has the same width and height as the Descending Passage. This low Ascending Passage continues for 1485 inches and ends, abruptly, where it opens into the Grand Gallery, a magnificent chamber, extending at the same angle, far up into the interior of the Pyramid.

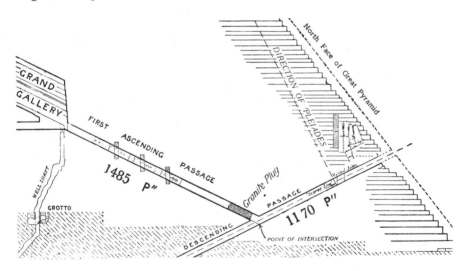

Originally covered over by the floor stones of the Grand Gallery is a long horizontal passage starting from the lower end of the Grand Gallery and terminating in the Queen's Chamber, beautifully constructed in limestone. The floor of this Chamber rests on the 25th course of masonry, from the base, of the Pyramid and is approximately 19 feet long and 17 feet wide. The height of the north

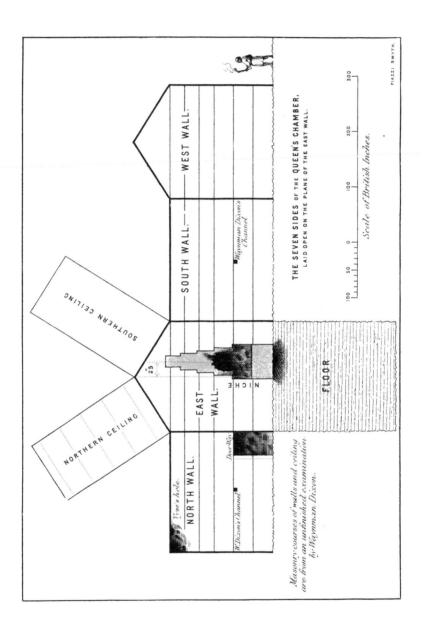

THE SEVEN SIDES OF THE QUEEN'S CHAMBER,
LAID OPEN ON THE PLANE OF THE EAST WALL.

Scale of British Inches.

300   200   100   0   50   100

PIAZZI SMYTH.

WEST WALL.

SOUTH WALL.

Wayman Dixon's Channel

SOUTHERN CEILING

NORTHERN CEILING

EAST WALL.

NICHE

FLOOR

NORTH WALL.

Doorway

Vyse's hole.

W. Dixon's Channel

*Masonry courses of walls and ceiling
are from an unfinished examination
by Wayman Dixon.*

and south walls is nearly 15 feet. The east and west walls are gabled, the apexes extending about 5 feet above the level ot the top of the north and south walls and about 20 feet above the floor of the Chamber.

It is recorded that the Queen's Chamber originally contained an empty coffer. Some of the limestone fragments now filling the many holes and corners of the chamber, caused by excavations, may possibly have come from the coffer.

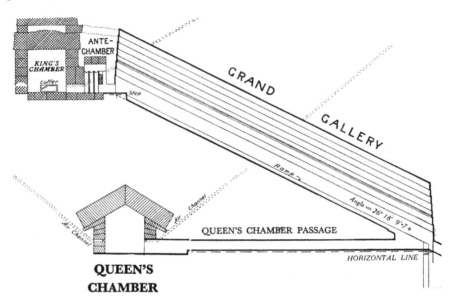

The Grand Gallery, sloping upward at the same gradient as the Ascending Passage, has two ramps, one on each side, running its full length. On the top surface of each ramp, at regular distances, oblong holes are cut vertically down - against the side walls. There are 28 such nitches on each ramp, however one on the west ramp is missing due to the forced opening from the Grotto to the Grand Gallery.

Having a length of 156 ¾ feet and a height of over 28 feet, the Grand Gallery exhibits the greatest and finest example of corbelled architecture extant. Seven feet wide,above the side ramps, the four walls rise, by means of seven overhanging courses of masonry, to a ceiling width of three and one half feet, the same as that of the floor. The projected masonry, averaging three inches beyond the course on which it rests, forms a corbel vault of unparalleled dimensions.

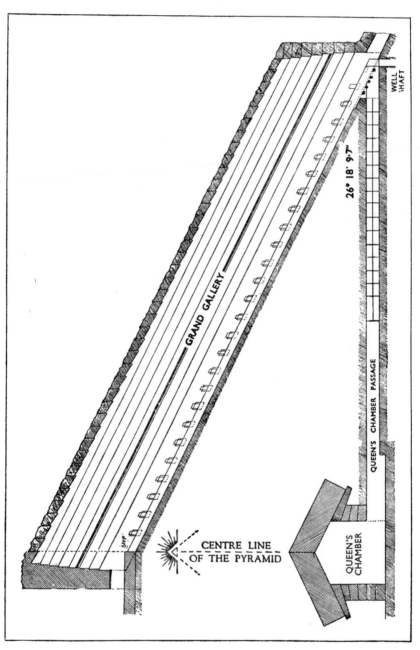

GRAND GALLERY and QUEEN'S CHAMBER PASSAGE

WELL SHAFT

26° 18' 9.7"

QUEEN'S CHAMBER PASSAGE

GRAND GALLERY

STEP

CENTRE LINE
OF THE PYRAMID

QUEEN'S
CHAMBER

Perret and Chipiez, renowned architects, in their work "Ancient Egyptian Art" state - "The glory of the workmen who built the Great Pyramid is the masonry of the Grand Gallery...The faces of the blocks of limestone of which the walls are composed have been dressed with such care that it is not surpassed even by the most perfect example of Hellenic architecture on the Acropolis at Athens."

THE GRAND GALLERY

The limestone walls of the Grand Gallery, which exhibit such excellent workmanship, are now much decayed and exfoliated, having been exposed to the air and the fumes from torches through many long centuries.

It is interesting to note that not only is the passage east of the Pyramid's north-south axis 286.1 inches, but the height of the Grand Gallery exceeds that of the Ascending Passage by that same figure. Also the perimeter of the platform, made to receive the capstone, was too short by that same measurement.

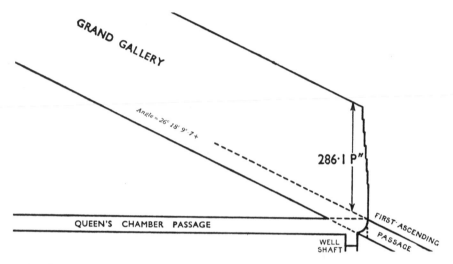

At the upper end of the Grand Gallery is the Great Step, having a height of 35.76277 P. inches and lying on the east-west axis of the Pyramid; that is to say, it is exactly half way through the Pyramid from north to south. The top of the Great Step which extends across the full width of the Grand Gallery is horizontal, and at the same level as the floor of the King's Chamber and passage.

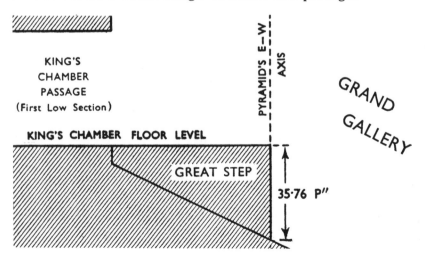

The horizontal King's Passage is divided into three sections (1) the First Low Section, (2) the High Central Section or so-called Ante-Chamber, and (3) the Second Low Section.

A Cross-Section of the Horizontal Passage System, showing:—
(1) The Great Step, (2) The First Low Passage, (3) The Ante-Chamber,
(4) The Second Low Passage, (5) The King's Chamber.

The southern end of the First Low Section emerges into what is commonly called the "Ante-Chamber". Its two side walls and south wall (except for one foot at the top) are of granite, cut and polished with exacting care. Each of the two side walls have a wainscot of approximately a foot thick. Thus the width of the Ante-Chamber is about two feet wider in its upper than in its lower part.

Each wainscot is characterized by four broad vertical grooves, 3-1/4 inches deep; those on the side walls (east and west) are exactly opposite one another. Three of these groves run from top to bottom of the wainscot and sink 3 inches below the floor-level. One, the most northerly, runs from the top down to the bottom of two granite slabs, one over the other, extending across the passage from wall to wall. These slabs together are known as the "Granite Leaf".

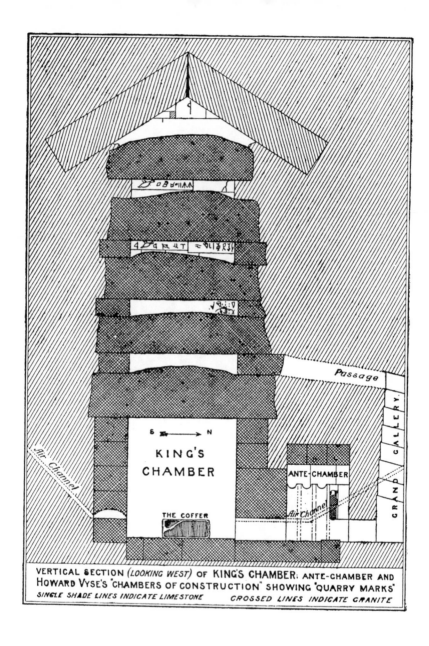

VERTICAL SECTION (*LOOKING WEST*) OF **KING'S CHAMBER**, ANTE-CHAMBER AND HOWARD VYSE'S "CHAMBERS OF CONSTRUCTION" SHOWING "QUARRY MARKS"
SINGLE SHADE LINES INDICATE LIMESTONE   *CROSSED LINES INDICATE GRANITE*

THE KING'S CHAMBER
and
Construction Chambers
(Looking West)

(The Coffer is not in its original position.)

The whole height of the Ante-Chamber from floor to ceiling measures approximately twelve and a half feet. The ceiling of the chamber is formed of three large blocks of granite which lie east-west. At the beginning or northern end of the chamber, the floor (for the first 13.22729 P. inches) is limestone. The remainder of the floor is red granite which continues on through the Second Low Section.

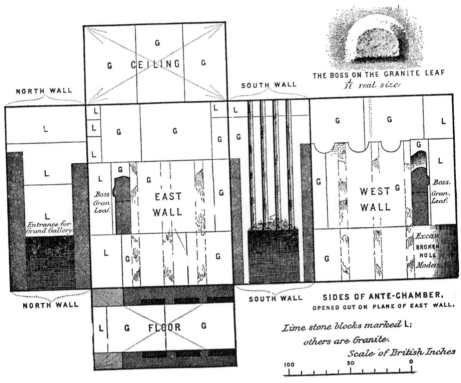

THE BOSS ON THE GRANITE LEAF
½ real size

SIDES OF ANTE-CHAMBER,
OPENED OUT ON PLANE OF EAST WALL.

Lime stone blocks marked L;
others are Granite.

Scale of British Inches

The object of interest in the Ante-Chamber is a raised Boss or Seal in the shape of a horseshoe, the center filled in solidly. This projection measures precisely five Pyramid inches across its face. This is exactly one-fifth of a Pyramid Sacred Cubit (25 P. inches). Again, the Sacred Cubit is indicated in that the edge of the Boss is precisely that distance (25 P. inches) from the eastern end of the Leaf. The Pyramid inch is demonstrated by the thickness of the Boss, which is raised that distance above the face of the Leaf, and by the fact that the Boss is exactly one P. inch from its center. The Sacred Cubit is also found demonstrated in stone in the Queen's Chamber. (The Sacred Cubit will be explained under geometric features on page 49).

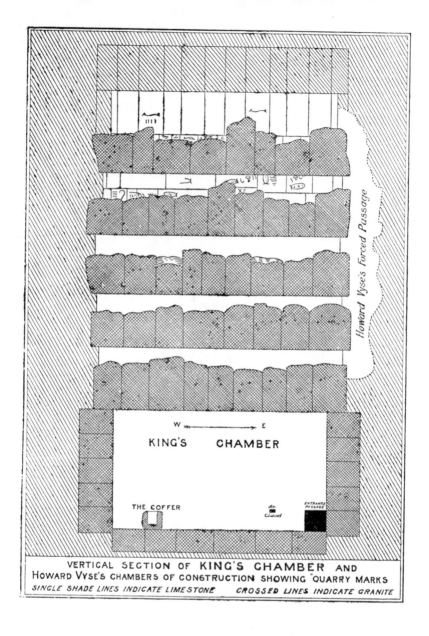

VERTICAL SECTION OF KING'S CHAMBER AND
HOWARD VYSE'S CHAMBERS OF CONSTRUCTION SHOWING QUARRY MARKS
SINGLE SHADE LINES INDICATE LIMESTONE   *CROSSED LINES INDICATE GRANITE*

THE KING'S CHAMBER
and
Construction Chambers
(Looking North)

(The Coffer is not in its original position.)

The Kings Chamber Passage ends in the King's Chamber, a spacious room of polished red granite approximately 34 feet long, 17 feet wide, and 19 feet high. Its roof is constructed of 43 massive beams, each 27 feet long and weighing from 50 to 70 tons; the beams are set joist-wise in five cushioned tiers and extend five feet beyond the walls. Above these are 24 great limestone rafters, forming a gabled roof. (See dia. pg. 38)

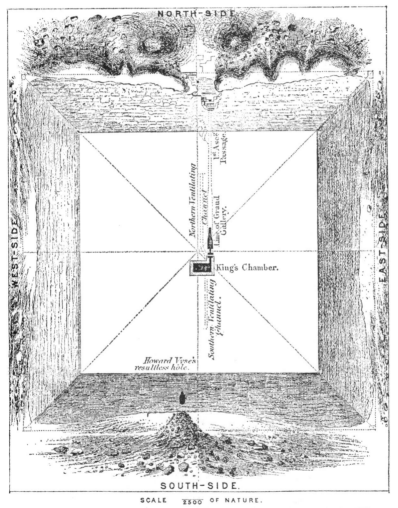

**HORIZONTAL SECTION OF THE GREAT PYRAMID
AT KING'S CHAMBER FLOOR-LEVEL**
(100 years-old drawing by Prof. C. Piazzi Smyth)

Above the roof of the King's Chamber are found a series of 5 cavities. These areas are appropriately termed "relieving chambers" by Egyptologists since the spaces have successfully prevented the collapse of the King's Chamber from the tremendous weight of the superincumbent masonry above the chamber area, amounting to several millions of tons.

One other feature should be noted. While the stones which supported the ends of the granite ceiling beams of the King's Chamber and of the lower Chambers of Construction are of granite, the upper supporting stones are limestones. This allows the upper supporting stones to take up any shock or subsidence caused by the great weight above them, by crushing, thus precluding any movement and subsidence from being communicated to the chamber's beneath.

That the design has proven successful is borne out by the fact that, even as it is, every one of the nine great granite beams forming the ceiling of the King's Chamber is cracked right across. Some of the granite beams above are also fractured and the huge sloping limestone rafters have been forced apart at the apex to the extent of 1 to 1½ inches.

The King's Chamber has two ventilators, one in the north wall, the other directly opposite in the south wall. Two air-channels were also found in the Queen's Chamber although they were not originally pierced through to the surface of the masonry. Each of the ventilator shafts were cut through each separate stone and laid throughout their slanting length out to the surface of the structure. These afforded a supply of fresh air to those parts of the Pyramid.

ENTRANCE DOORWAY and N. VENTILATOR

In four of the five shallow relieving spaces over the King's Chamber roof can be seen the only original hieroglyphics to be found anywhere in the Pyramid. None of these hieroglyphics, however, are inscribed in the stone itself but are written in red paint; being quarry marks by the ancient builders. Their importance lies in the fact that they reveal the Great Pyramid was built during the reign of Khufu and that its erection had reached the stage of constructing these "chambers" in the 17th year of his reign.

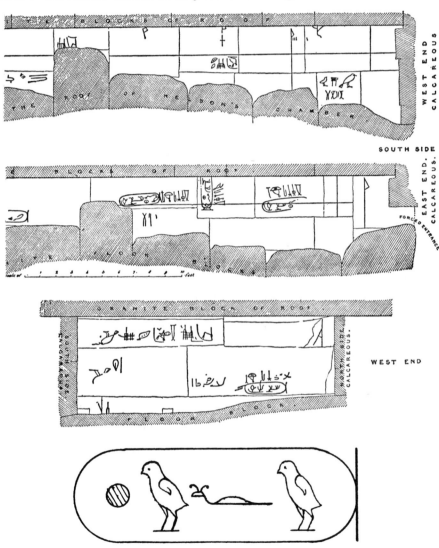

CARTOUCHE OF KHUFU

Just as modern shipbuilders and others work to carefully prepared patterns, so, it appears, the builders of the Great Pyramid had a pattern cut into the rock to guide them when arranging the passage-system of their huge monument. This rock-cut pattern, which is situated about a hundred yards east of the Great Pyramid, has been named the "Trial Passages".

With the single exception of the position of the Well-shaft, these passages are an exact model of the Great Pyramid's passage-system, shortened in length, but of full size in width and height. The resemblance is striking, even to the beginning of the Horizontal Passage to the Queen's Chamber, the ramps at the sides of the Grand Gallery, and the contraction at the lower end of the Ascending Passage to hold the Granite Plug. However, the contraction occurs additionally in the height, as well as in the width of the Ascending Passage.

Although we do find the vertical shaft is in a different position in the Trial Pssages, it is evidently intended as a model of the Well-shaft in the Great Pyramid, the bore of each being the same. The total lengths of the Descending and Ascending Passages are 66 feet and 50 feet respectively.

COFFER

Although the Queen's Chamber is known to have had an empty sarcophagus, the sarcophagus, or Coffer, found today, in the western end of the King's Chamber, is the only movable object in the Great Pyramid. It is of a type used in Egypt at the time the Pyramid was built, but is neither inscribed nor decorated as was the custom of the day. When discovered, it was found empty.

The top is grooved around its inner top edges as though to receive a lid, but there is no evidence that the Coffer ever had a lid. These facts, together with the venting of the chamber by the ventilators, would seem to indicate that it was not intended to be a tomb. That it never was used as a tomb is confirmed by the statements of the classical historians, Herodotus and Diodorus, that Cheops (Khufu) was buried elsewhere.

Since the Coffer is too large to pass through the low passages leading into the King's Chamber, it had to have been placed in the chamber before the chamber was closed and the passages sealed.

The Coffer is formed from a single piece of red Aswan granite and exhibits an amazing feat of workmanship. It was hollowed out as a carpenter might hollow out a block of wood with an auger. The spiral markings on the inner sides can still be discerned. Engineers have estimated that to accomplish this feat it would require an overhead pressure of from one to two tons and the bits would have to have been a very hard and tough material, likely some precious stone.

Geometrically the Coffer is 89.80568 inches long, 38.69843 inches wide and 41.21319 inches high in its exterior measurements. The sum of the length, width and height of the Coffer is equal to 1/5 of the sum of the length, width and height of the King's Chamber itself. The sides are close to 6 inches thick and the bottom 7 inches.

The cubic volume of the walls and bottom of the Coffer is approximately equal to the contents it could hold. This capacity is equal to four British quarters, the established measure of wheat. Measures of capacity are the sources of measures of weight and a capacity and the Avoirdupois pound. The Pyramid's Coffer appears to have furnished the standard of all measures of capacity to the earliest Greek nations as well as the Hebrew. It is interesting to note that the English speaking nations use a system of weights and measures more closely related to this early standard.

The Coffer, in the King's Chamber,

South — North

Elevation, looking West.

West

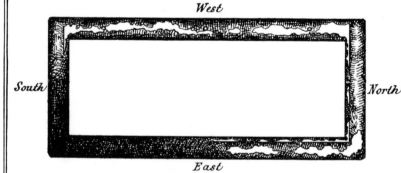

South — North

East

Plan, looking from above.

*the shading in proportion to the deviation
from a horizontal plane.*

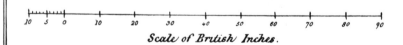

10 5 0   10   20   30   40   50   60   70   80   90

Scale of British Inches.

The capacity of the Coffer is also equal to that of the Ark of the Covenant in the Biblical Tabernacle and the measure of the Molten Sea of Solomon's Temple was exactly fifty times this capacity and also equal to the measure of the King's Chamber itself.

There is also noted a correspondency between the King's Chamber and the Holy of Holies and between the Ante-Chamber and the place called Holy in the Bible Tabernacle. These significant correspondencies seem to suggest that the designers of each must have had a common source of inspiration.

In its original position, the Coffer sat midway between the north and the south walls of the King's Chamber with its sides parallel to the respective sides of the Chamber and its axis coinciding with the Pyramid's own north-south axis. That is to say that the Coffer's axis, which was due north and south, would be geometrically 286.1 inches west of the axis of the passage system.

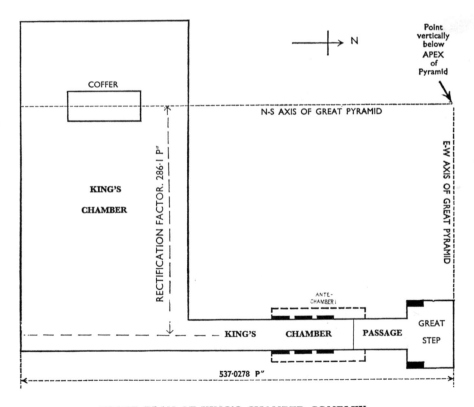

FLOOR PLAN OF KING'S CHAMBER COMPLEX

THE "COFFER" IN THE KING'S CHAMBER

GEOMETRIC CONSTRUCTION

An ancient treatise on Masonry (The legend of the Craft) states that all sciences are founded upon one science and that science is Geometry. Few persons, not conversant with geometry, recognize the great usefulness of geometrical reasoning, or realize how much it enters into modern technology, especially engineering.

The Great Pyramid is, internally, and externally, geometrical in conception and design. For this reason the problem of the Great Pyramid is essentially one to be solved, not by the Egyptologist as such, but by the engineer, since it has been erected on principles easily recognized and understood by the construction engineer.

Merely exploring the structure will reveal nothing as regards to its true purpose. A knowledge of geometry and mathematics, therefore, combined with an understanding of their proper application, is essential to a correct understanding of the Great Pyramid and its design.

It is not by hieroglyphics nor by sculpture work, but by symbol, measure and angle, that the Great Pyramid of Giza, in the land of Egypt, yields its secret.

Scientifically directed surveys have furnished the actual geometric measurements of the Pyramid. From these measurements calculated data was obtained which revealed the Great Pyramid to constitute a geometrical representation, on a vast scale, of mathematical and astronomical knowledge not to be known, again, for over 4500 years. The remarkable manner in which this knowledge is geometrically expressed, relative to certain simple mathematical formulae, surpasses in every way, any similar undertaking of man.

The unit of measure employed in the actual construction of the Great Pyramid was the Egyptian Royal Cubit. However, the linear unit predominating in the design of the Pyramid is the Sacred Cubit, which is shown on the Boss in the Ante-Chamber. A scientific examination of the Sacred Cubit found it to bear an exact relationship to the size of the planet on which we live. This Cubit is the exact 10,000,000th part of the distance from the center of the earth to the pole, or semi-axis. According to the results of the latest geodetic research in the International Geophysical Year 1957-1958, the polar radius of the earth, as deduced from observations of the orbits of artificial satellites, is approximately 3949.89 miles. Divide

49

this figure by 10,000,000; the result is 1 Sacred Cubit (25 Pyramid inches) or 25,0265 British inches. *

Thus the earth's polar radius measures 10,000,000 Sacred Cubits or 250,000,000 Pyramid inches; hence the Pyramid inch is the 500,000,000th part of the earth's polar diameter.

---

* When the Pilgrim Fathers and early British settlers went out to America, they took the British system of weights and measures with them; but already in the U.S.A. these have deviated slightly from the original. Expressed in units of the metric system the British Inch is equivalent to 25.399978 mm., whilst the present U.S.A. Inch is 25.400051 mm. International Industries have, however, unofficially adopted an Inch of 25.4 mm.

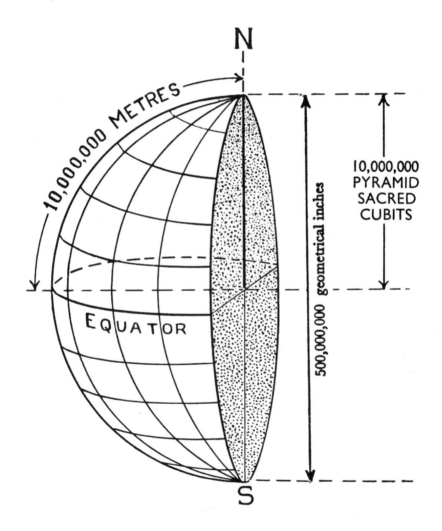

If this method of arriving at a measure of distance seems unusual, consider the French metre, conceived as a unit of linear measure based also upon the size of the earth. The French metre was arrived at by taking the 10,000,000th part of the so-called "quadrant of the earth" as calculated from the North Pole to the equator, along a meridian passing through Dunkirk. As the earth is not a perfect sphere, the said distance is not a true quadrant, hence it is not truly scientific to determine a unit of straight measure from such a surface.The calculations were subsequently found to be slightly in error. Thus the Designer of the Great Pyramid long forestalled modern man in the scientific idea of having a unit of measure based on the size of the earth, and therefore knew the exact dimensions of the earth.

It is amazing to what a small extent the original perfect inch, as still preserved in the Great Pyramid, has fluctuated down through the ages. The inch as now used in Britain, after all these long centuries, only deviates from the original scientific standard by approximately a thousandth part of an inch. The U.S.A. inch, differing insignificantly from the British inch, may be regarded as being practically identical. As we go back into history, we find that the British inch deviated even less from the original true scientific inch of the Great Pyramid, and it is not unlikely that it was derived from it.

It is worthy of special note that the entire geometric structure of the Great Pyramid is designed on the basis of π (pi), 3.14159, the mathematical ratio upon which the whole physical universe is designed, and the value of y, 365.242, the number of days in Earth's solar year, (the time interval in days between two successive vernal equinoxes in the earth's journey around the sun).

In mathematics, π (sixteenth letter of the Greek alphabet) is the ratio between the circumference of a circle and its diameter (the straight line through its center). That is to say, the circumference of any size circle is always 3.14159 times its diameter. This sign has been adopted because of the fact that the ratio in question has never been ascertained to its finality, although of course, it has been calculated to an exceedingly high degree of precision. namely, to over 5,000 decimal places (To 15 places of decimals π is 3.141592653589793).

The amazing fact that this geometric ratio π , which pervades the whole universe, from the vast solar systems to the tiniest atoms, also pervades the Great Pyramid, was first revealed by the

Geometric Construction of the Great Pyramid

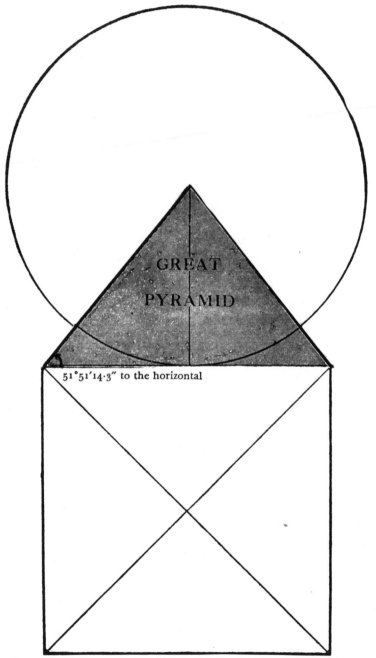

GREAT

PYRAMID

51°51′14·3″ to the horizontal

Circumference of the Circle = Perimeter of the Square

angle of the slope of the Pyramid's sides. This angle results in the Pyramid's vertical height bearing the same ratio to the perimeter of its base that the radius of a circle bears to the circumference. (See dia. pg. 52).

In other words, if the height of the Pyramid to its apex be taken as the radius of a circle, the distance around the Pyramid is found to be exactly equal to the circumference of that circle. The required angle of the slope of the Pyramid's sides to produce this result is consequently known as the pyramidic π angle and is 51° 51' 14.3". No other pyramid in the world is built at this angle.

Although the squaring of a circle is an insoluble problem, if we use the incommensurable number of π, the Pyramid's design, for all practical purposes, accomplished the squaring of the circle.

Nearly all the dimensions of the interior (and the Architect's design of the exterior) are expressible in terms of the length of the solar year. The square base circuit of the Pyramid equals 36,524,235 inches.

The floor of the King's Chamber is the 35th course of masonry (50 inches in thickness which is thicker than those above or below it. This course extends, from its outside edge to the center vertical line, a distance of 3,652.423 inches. It is also 1162.6 inches above the base, and at this height its perimeter measures 8 times 3652.42 inches; so that a rectangle is defined as 3652.4 inches by 1162.6 inches. This rectangle defines the Ancient Egyptian unit of land area known as an "Aroura."

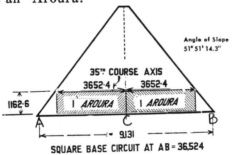

The measurements of the interior chambers reveal the length of the Ante-Chamber to be 116.26025 inches. Multiplying that figure by 25 (The Sacred Cubit) and again by π, equals the base side length of the Pyramid. The Ante-Chamber length, multiplied by π, alone, equals 365.2423 inches. The distance from the exact center of the

Ante-Chamber to the south wall of the King's Chamber is also 365.24235 inches.

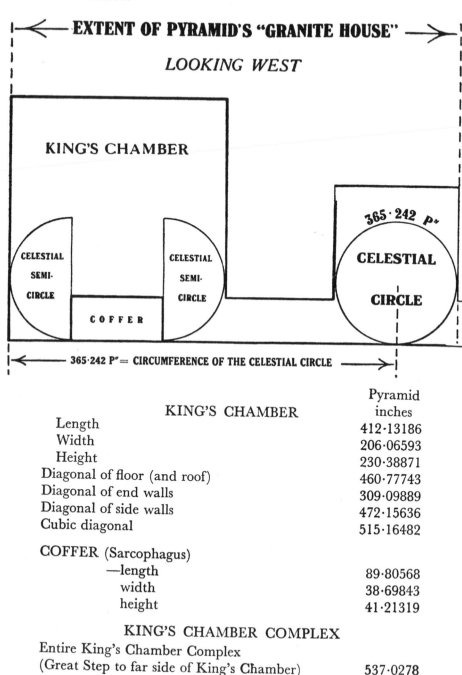

EXTENT OF PYRAMID'S "GRANITE HOUSE"

LOOKING WEST

KING'S CHAMBER

CELESTIAL SEMI-CIRCLE

CELESTIAL SEMI-CIRCLE

365·242 P″

CELESTIAL CIRCLE

COFFER

365·242 P″ = CIRCUMFERENCE OF THE CELESTIAL CIRCLE

	Pyramid inches
KING'S CHAMBER	
Length	412·13186
Width	206·06593
Height	230·38871
Diagonal of floor (and roof)	460·77743
Diagonal of end walls	309·09889
Diagonal of side walls	472·15636
Cubic diagonal	515·16482
COFFER (Sarcophagus)	
—length	89·80568
width	38·69843
height	41·21319

KING'S CHAMBER COMPLEX

Entire King's Chamber Complex (Great Step to far side of King's Chamber)	537·0278

Twice the length of the King's Chamber in Pyramid inches, taken in conjunction with the angle of the passages which leads up to it, also indicates the period of the earth's revolution round the sun. In other words, the length of the King's Chamber (412.132 x 2) be marked off on the floor of the ascending passages, and a right-angled triangle be formed by drawing a perpendicular and base-line from the upper and lower extremities respectively of this portion of the floor, the perpendicular will be found to measure exactly the number of days in the solar year, or 365.242 in Pyramid inches.

Yet another method by which the King's Chamber shows its connection with the solar year is to take the length of the King's Chamber (412.132 P. inches) to express the diameter of a circle. Compute, by the best methods of modern science, the area of that circle: throw that area into a square shape, and find the length of a side of such square. The answer will be 365.242 inches.

The Geometric measurements can be seen, in all cases, as simple geometrical functions of the year-circle, the latter being a circle whose circumference, in Pyramid inches, is 100 times the number of days in the solar year.

The form, arrangement and detail of the Pyramid's exterior, and of its interior passages and chambers, can therefore be built up entirely from the geometry of the year-circle. This fact implies the possession of a knowledge of mathematics, geometry and astronomy, combined with the ability to express them in structural form, far in advance of contemporary knowledge of that time.

In the design of the Pyramid is found a unique geometrical symbolism so profound as to transcend anything that human ingenuity might devise. (For details the reader is referred to Pyramidology Book No. 1, by Adam Rutherford).

From the level of the top of the Great Step and King's Chamber floor up to the summit platform there are 153 courses of masonry. (See also footnote on page 174 of Book I.) The significance of the wonderful number 153 greatly interests both Bible students and Pyramid students. The fact that on the memorable occasion of the great draught of fishes, recorded in John 21,[11], the number is not given in round figures as, about 150, but stated precisely as 153, infers a special reason for this and indicates that the number has a special significance. At the outset it is interesting to note the mathematical feature that 153 is the sum of all whole numbers from 1 to 17:

$$1+2+3+4+5+6+7+8+9+10+11+12+13+14+15+16+17 = 153$$

or expressed algebraically:

$$\frac{n}{2}(a+l) = \frac{17}{2}(1+17) = 153.$$

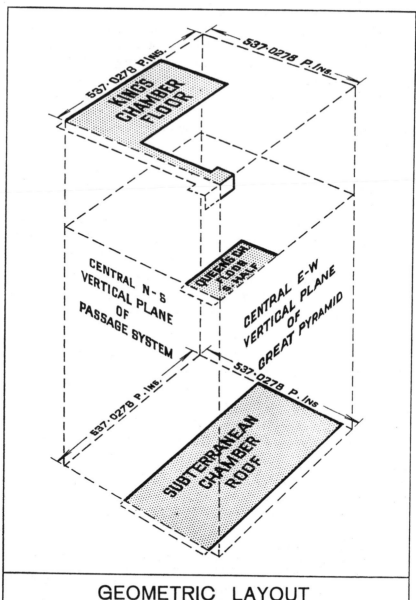

GEOMETRIC LAYOUT
OF THE
PRINCIPAL CHAMBERS
IN THE
GREAT PYRAMID

MATHEMATICAL PROPORTIONS

Ancient Egypt seems to possess, to a remarkable degree, an advanced knowledge of mathematics and kindred sciences, but they were never able to duplicate the proportionate mathematic system of numbers, found in the design of the Great Pyramid.

Having been shown how to build the ideal pyramid, and with the perfect model before them, they could copy it externally. However, all subsequent pyramids show a steadily deteriorating standard of construction.

An example of the symmetry of mathematical proportions in the Great Pyramid is found in the measurements of the King's Chamber and Ante-Chamber. Their dimensions show that:

1. The breadth of the King's Chamber, equals half its length.

2. The height of the King's Chamber, equals half the diagonal of its floor.

3. The length of the granite portion of the Ante-Chamber floor, is equal to half the breadth of the King's Chamber.

4. The length of the granite portion of the Ante-Chamber floor, multiplied by 5 (a special Pyramid number), equals the solid cubic diagonal of the King's Chamber.

5. The length of the granite portion of the Ante-Chamber floor, multiplied by 50, equals the length of the side of a square, the area of which equals the area of a triangle of the shape and size of the Pyramid's right section.

6. The length of the King's Chamber, multiplied by 25 (a Pyramid cubit), equals an even 100 times the length of the Ante-Chamber's granite floor.

7. If the length of the granite portion of the Ante-Chamber floor be multiplied by an even 100, and this length be taken to express the diameter of a circle, the arc of that circle will be found to equal the arc of the square base of the Pyramid.

8. The height of the Ante-Chamber, multiplied by an even 100, equals the base side length, plus the vertical height, of the Pyramid.

9. The Ante-Chamber length, multiplied by 50, equals the vertical height of the Pyramid.

The Pyramid's Sacred Cubit itself is comprised of 25 (5 times 5 inches) inches and this inch is the 500,000,000th part of the Earth's axis of rotation (polar axis).

Although an examination shows that the Pyramid numerics are geometric, there is one arithmetical number that is prominent in the Pyramid, and that number is 5. The number 5, and multiples, powers and geometrical proportions of it runs through the Great Pyramid and its measure references. The floor of the Queen's Chamber is 5 times 5 courses of masonry from the base upwards and its measures all answer to a standard of 5 times 5 inches. The King's Chamber floor is 10 times 5 courses from the base and its walls are composed of 20 times 5 stones, arranged in 5 horizontal courses. The Pyramid itself has 5 corners (four at the base and one at the apex) and hence it has 5 sides; four equal triangular sides and the square under-side on which it stands. The name pyramid*comes from the Coptic word "pyr" which means division and the word "met" which means ten thus suggesting the number 5.

Periods of 5 years are the integral units with which the whole structure of prophetic chronology is built up, in the Bible. The Prophetic chronological numbers 5, 10, 15, 40, 65, 70, 100, 120, 360, 390, 400, 490, 1000, 1260, 1290, 1335, 2300 and the "Seven Times" (2520 years) are all multiples of 5.

The number 5 symbolizes "Grace". Four is the number of this world (man) plus one, Divine Power (God). "Number in Scripture" by Bullinger. Multiples of 5 were also the dimensions of Noah's Ark, the Wilderness Tabernacle and Solomon's Temple.

A remarkable mathematical relationship between the Great Pyramid and the original verses in Isaiah 19: 19-20, which were written in Hebrew, was found when it was noted that the actual height of the Pyramid, as left by the builders, was 5449 inches. The sum total of the numerical value of the Hebrew text of Isaiah 19: 19-20 is 5449 (See chart Pg. 59). The distance from the Pyramids entrance right through to the farthest extremity of the interior passages and chambers is also equal to 5449 inches.

* DERIVATIVES FROM THE WORD "PYRAMID"

PYRAMIDAL, PYRAMIDALISM, PYRAMIDALIST, PYRAMIDALLY, PYRAMIDATE, PYRAMIDATED, PYRAMIDIA, PYRAMIDIC, PYRAMID-ICAL, PYRAMIDICALLY, PYRAMIDION, PYRAMIDIST, PYRAMIDIZE, PYRAMIDIZATION, PYRAMIDO-ATTENUATE, PYRAMIDO-PRIS-, MATIC, PYRAMIDOGRAPHIA, PYRAMIDOGRAPHY, PYRAMIDOID, PYRAMIDOIDAL, PYRAMIDOLOGY, PYRAMIDOLOGIST, PYRAMIDY, PYRAMOID, PYRAMOIDAL.

The Great Pyramid Text of Scripture

—— Isaiah 19: 19-20 ——

ביום ההוא יהיה מזבח ליהוה בתוך ארץ מצרים ומצבה
אצל-גבולה ליהוה : והיה לאות ולעד ליהוה צבאות
בארץ מצרים כי-יצעקו אל-יהוה מפני לחצים וישלח
להם מושיע ורב והצילם :

This Great Pyramid Text of Scripture, in the original Hebrew, contains 30 words. In Hebrew the letters of the alphabet were employed as arithmetical figures, consequently every word is also a row of figures and thus all Hebrew writing has numeric value. The above Hebrew Text as numbers is as shown below—the value of every letter is given and each line represents a word. **The total value is 5,449.**

(1)	2 +	10 +	6 +	40						=	58
(2)	5 +	5 +	6 +	1						=	17
(3)	10 +	5 +	10 +	5						=	30
(4)	40 +	7 +	2 +	8						=	57
(5)	30 +	10 +	5 +	6 +	5					=	56
(6)	2 +	400 +	6 +	20						=	428
(7)	1 +	200 +	90							=	291
(8)	40 +	90 +	200 +	10 +	40					=	380
(9)	6 +	40 +	90 +	2 +	5					=	143
(10)	1 +	90 +	30							=	121
(11)	3 +	2 +	6 +	30 +	5					=	46
(12)	30 +	10 +	5 +	6 +	5					=	56
(13)	6 +	5 +	10 +	5						=	26
(14)	30 +	1 +	6 +	400						=	437
(15)	6 +	30 +	70 +	4						=	110
(16)	30 +	10 +	5 +	6 +	5					=	56
(17)	90 +	2 +	1 +	6 +	400					=	499
(18)	2 +	1 +	200 +	90						=	293
(19)	40 +	90 +	200 +	10 +	40					=	380
(20)	20 +	10								=	30
(21)	10 +	90 +	70 +	100 +	6					=	276
(22)	1 +	30								=	31
(23)	10 +	5 +	6 +	5						=	26
(24)	40 +	80 +	50 +	10						=	180
(25)	30 +	8 +	90 +	10 +	40					=	178
(26)	6 +	10 +	300 +	30 +	8					=	354
(27)	30 +	5 +	40							=	75
(28)	40 +	6 +	300 +	10 +	70					=	426
(29)	6 +	200 +	2							=	208
(30)	6 +	5 +	90 +	10 +	30 +	40			=	181

Height of the Great Pyramid in Pyramid inches = 5,449

(to the original Summit Platform)

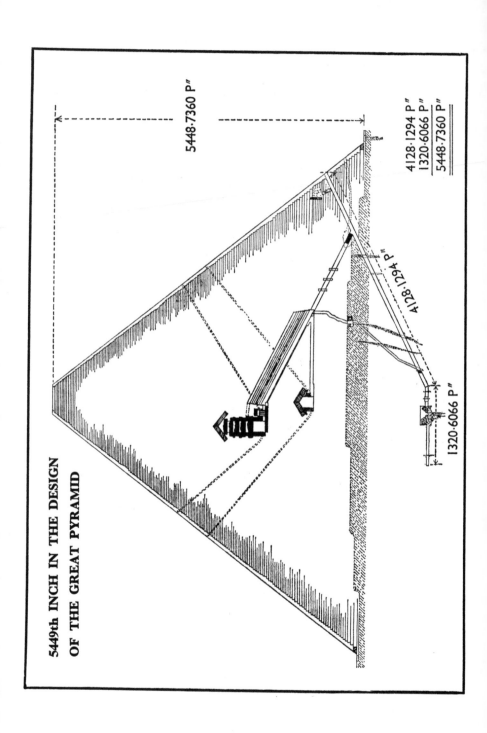

5449th INCH IN THE DESIGN
OF THE GREAT PYRAMID

5448·7360 P″

4128·1294 P″
1320·6066 P″
5448·7360 P″

4128·1294 P″

1320·6066 P″

SCIENTIFIC FEATURES

Many features of the Great Pyramid exhibit design on the part of the Architect to embody relative scientific time and distance measurements in parts of the structure where they could not be overlooked. A few will be mentioned here, but only in briefest detail:

(1) The sun's distance from the earth: For over 2,500 years man has struggled to solve this problem. The Greeks in 500 B.C. judged the distance to be about ten miles, later guessing it to be more like 2,000 miles. In later centuries man estimated it farther and farther away, until in the 16th century it had increased to 36,000,000 miles. The latest figures of modern astronomy give 92,900,00 miles as the sun's mean distance from the earth. As there was absolutely no way of calculating this until recently, scientists were astounded to discover that built into the Great Pyramid's base plans was a figure approximating 92,000,000 miles.

The problem involved the discovery of the proper scale. It was known that the four lines from the corner sockets to the apex of the Great Pyramid sloped inward 10 feet for every 9 feet of elevation. This suggested a possible equation. Multiplying the height of the Pyramid by 10, nine times, and reducing the result to miles, gave the astonishing result of 91,856,060 miles.

(2) The mean density of the earth: The true mean density or specific gravity of the earth has also been an age-old problem. An average of prominent tests has placed it at 5,672 times the weight of water at 68 degrees Fahrenheit. The Pyramid places it at 5.7, a figure closely approximating the average estimates.

(3) The weight of the earth: Knowing the density of the earth enabled physicists to ascertain its weight to be approximately 5,300,000,000,000,000,000,000, (U.S.A. about six billion trillion) tons. The earth's weight and the weight of the Pyramid were found to be proportionately related to one another. The Pyramid's weight of approximately 5,300,000 tons has been noted to be 1,000,000,000,000,000 (U.S.A. one thousand trillionth) the weight of the earth. It is not unreasonable to assume that the Architect used this proportion to indicate the weight of the earth.

(4) Volume of the earth's crust above mean sea-level: The vast amount of surveying necessary to determine the average height of all the land on earth would have been an impossible task even a few

hundred years ago. With the advent of aerial photography and the accumulation of data from continuing geological surveys, together with modern computers, an estimate is now given as approximately 455 feet. The top of the Pyramid, as the builders left it unfinished, is fully 454½ feet.

(5) Mean ocean level of the earth: The mean ocean level was found to approximate 193 feet 7 inches below the baseline of the Great Pyramid. Again, modern computers and the findings of modern oceanography were required to ascertain this figure. And again the design of the Great Pyramid foretold this fact. It was found that taking twice the diameter (1,162.6") of a circle having a circumference of 3,652.42" (a circle again related to the solar year and base circuit of the Pyramid) gave a result of 2325.2", or just slightly over 193 feet 7 inches. This ancient wonder in architecture based upon the geometry of the year cycle is shown to be in harmony with the earth's design.

(6) Mean temperature of the earth: As the Great Pyramid stands on the line which equally divides the surface of the northern hemisphere, there is a relationship between its climate and the mean temperature of all the earth's surface. This temperature is about 68 degrees Fahrenheit. In the Pyramid this temperature is maintained permanently and unvaryingly in the King's Chamber. Two air channels, when cleaned of sand, were found to keep this chamber at the normal of mean temperature, which temperature is exactly one fifth of the distance between the freezing and boiling points of water. Scientists say that 68 degrees Fahrenheit is the ideal temperature for the existence of man.

(7) Rotundity of the earth: The rotundity, or curvature, of the earth was found by surveying the side baseline of the Pyramid. Due to the hollowed-in core masonry (35.76 inches on each side) a curved line was produced. Computations were made to ascertain how long the radius would be that would produce a circle containing that curve. The resulting answer was that the radius would be approximately half the diameter of the earth.

(8) Golden Rule of Architecture: The Great Pyramid conforms perfectly to the recognized laws of harmony and beauty. The Egyptians, Cretans, and Greeks all knew about the Golden Rule of Architecture, also called the "Golden Number." Such architectural masterpieces as the Parthenon on the Acropolis, at Athens, conformed to it, but not with the high degree of mathematical

precision to be found in the Pyramid built over 2,000 years earlier.

This "Golden Number", when worked out, turns out to be the cosine of the π angle of the Great Pyramid, expressed as correct to three decimal places, namely, .618; in other words, the ratio that the distance from the center of the Pyramid's base out to each of the four sides bears to the oblique height of the Pyramid's faces, is precisely the Architect's Golden Number, correct to three decimal places.

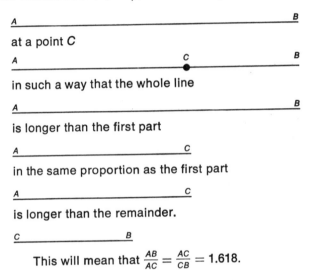

The Golden Section, or φ, is obtained by dividing a line

A ———————————————————————— B

at a point C

A ——————————————— C ———————— B

in such a way that the whole line

A ———————————————————————— B

is longer than the first part

A ——————————————— C

in the same proportion as the first part

A ——————————————— C

is longer than the remainder.

C ——————— B

This will mean that $\frac{AB}{AC} = \frac{AC}{CB} = 1.618$.

In the Great Pyramid the rectangular floor of the King's Chamber (which consists of two equal squares, or a 1 x 2 rectangle) also serves to illustrate and to obtain the Golden Section.

If you split one of two squares in half and swing the diagonal down to the base, the point where the diagonal touches the base will be φ or 1.618 in relation to the side of the square, which is 1. *

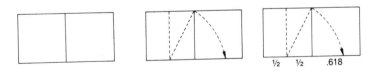

* Pythagoras' theorem will also show that the value of φ will be $1/2 + \sqrt{5/2}$, or 1.618, and that $\varphi - 1$ will be .618.

CONSTRUCTION OF THE GREAT PYRAMID'S BASE.

(Hollowing-in of core masonry GREATLY EXAGGERATED to show effect.)

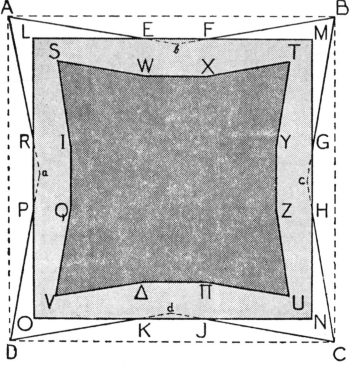

LMNO—Base as actually built. *
SWXTYZUΠΔVQI—Base of core masonry.

AB = 365.242 Sacred Cubits = Number of days in the solar year.
AEFB = 365.256 ,, ,, = ,, ,, ,, sidereal year.
AbB = 365.259 ,, ,, = ,, ,, ,, anomalistic year.
    The same arrangement holds good on all four sides of the Pyramid, hence the three complete circuits, ABCD, AEFBGHCJKDPR, AbBcCdDa also bear the same ratio to each other as the three astronomical years, i.e., 365.242 : 365.256 : 365.259 (For higher degree of precision, with values stated as correct to 5 places of decimals, see page 65).

* The side length of the Great Pyramid's base expressed in British feet is just over 755¾.

ASTRONOMICAL DESIGN

The base circuit of the Great Pyramid contains still a greater wonder. As our earth has three separate lengths of years, namely (1) the solar tropical year, (2) the sidereal year, and (3) the anomalistic year, just so were the baselines and walls of this Pyramid constructed, with three different lengths of circumferences.

The measurements designating the three astronomical years were found in the hollowed-in core masonry on the faces of the Pyramid. Hidden by the original straight planes of the exterior casing stones of the Pyramid, they would never have been revealed except for the removal of the casing stones. These different cycles have to do with the earth and its relation to both the stars and the sun.

The earth rotates on a plane inclined to the ecliptic. This motion from west to east every 24 hours gives us day and night and occurs at the rate of 1,000 miles per hour at the Equator. While spinning like a top the earth is also racing in its orbit around the sun anti-clockwise at the much higher rate of speed of 1,000 miles per minute. The tilt in the earth's axis causes the four seasons, from summer to summer. The solar year is the period wherein the sun appears to pass over the earth 365.24235 times or days between the Vernal Equinoxes.

The sidereal year is the interval between the earth's position at any time in the year, in relation to the fixed stars, and its return to that position. In other words, the star-heavens appear to pass over the earth 365.25636 times during the circuit. This difference of about 20 minutes is due to the earth's slow rotation clockwise, thus causing the solar tropical year to be shorter.

The anomalistic year is the interval between successive annual returns of the earth to the point – defined as the perihelion – in its orbit nearest the sun (Jan. 2-3). This requires 365.25986 days, or about five minutes longer than the sideral year, due to the motion of the earth's orbit.

This period of time varies, being greater or less depending on from what stage of its movement it is calculated. Modern science gives the cycle as approximately 25,800 years. It is noted that the sum of the two diagonals of the Pyramid's full designed base (12,913.27 pyramid inches) x 2 = 25,826.54, a figure considered by some scholars to represent the precessional cycle.

There are other remarkable examples of interlocking mathematical solar distances found in the design of the Pyramid, demonstrating the Architect to have preceeded modern astronomers by over 4000 years.

With regards to its astronomical position, it seems the builders intended to place the Pyramid as close as possible in latitude 30°, or, in other words, in that latitude where the true pole of the heavens is one-third of the way from the horizon to the point overhead (the zenith), and where the noon sun at true spring or autumn (when the sun rises almost exactly in the east, and sets almost exactly in the west) is two-thirds of the way from the horizon to the point overhead. Star observations, made from this position, would simplify many problems in the geometrical construction of the Pyramid.

That the Great Pyramid was constructed in accordance with astronomical observations of great accuracy is beyond doubt. And to achieve such exactness without modern scientific instruments is, seemingly, unbelievable.

The alignment of the Pyramid can be determined from a sighting of the Pole Star. This sighting could be accomplished by boring a slanting passage, in the solid rock, positioned so as to point to the Pole Star when due north. Such a boring exists beneath the base of the Pyramid, running some 350 feet through the solid rock (the lower portion of the Descending Passage). This passage is found to be in exact alignment with the true north.

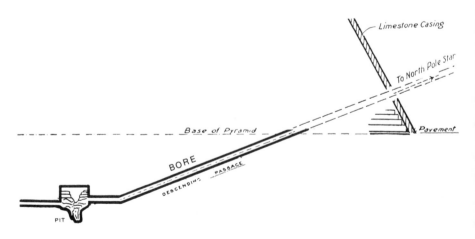

20TH CENTURY PROBES

In the hope of finding previously undiscovered passages and chambers in the Great Pyramid several methods have been used and from time to time others will, probably, be tried.

Sound waves and magnetism tests failed to produce satisfactory results. Cosmic ray probes, a system developed by Dr. Luis Alvarez, the 1968 Nobel Prize winner for physics, did prove to be successful although they failed to find any unknown chambers.

The device operates much like an X-ray machine, except the rays are generated in outer space and not by the machine. A spark chamber, when placed in a chamber in a pyramid, will measure the strength and direction of cosmic ray particles, which constantly bombard the earth and pass through such massive stone structures as pyramids. By analyzing countless rays, over several weeks, those that have passed through empty areas are located, tunnels can be dug, directly, to the open area.

In 1968, under the direction of D. Lauren Yazolino, Alvarez's assistant, two million cosmic ray trajectories made in the Second Pyramid (Cephren) had been measured and run through a computer, in Cairo, for analysis. Results indicated the system was working satisfactorily. Re-analysis of the tapes, however, produced different patterns which caused Dr. Amr Goneid, another scientist affiliated with the project to be quoted as saying,"It defies all known laws of physics" and "some force beyond man's comprehension was brought to bear on the readings."

Further checks, at Berkeley, Calif. by Dr. Avarez and Dr. Yazolino, showed the "mysterious readings" to be the result of the spark chamber running out of neon gas, and no other chambers than what is known to exist were found. Similar tests made later in the Great Pyramid also produced no indication of unknown chambers.

In 1974, a joint team from the Ain Shams University of Egypt and the Stanford Research Institute of California, U.S.A., carried out Electronmagnetic Sounder experiments at the Pyramids, again with the object of finding hidden chambers. This method, developed under the leadership of Professor Lambert T. Dolphin, utilized radio-wave propagation to detect chambers, instead of the cosmic ray method of Professor Alvarez.

The cosmic ray method was limited in that the detector, of necessity, must point in an upward direction and therefore cannot locate any chambers below its own position. The electromagnetic sounder method is not limited in this respect. It can be pointed in any direction, consequently in theory it should be more versatile.

The first test was to discover the actual in-situ losses in bedrock and in the core masonry of Chephren's Pyramid. Accordingly the apparatus was set up in the Lower Chamber and in "Belzoni's" Chamber, as well as half way up the North face of the pyramid. Much to everyone's surprise it was found that the energy loss in the bedrock was more than three times the expected level. In fact, no signals could be detected by the receiver over the 220 feet distance between the two chambers. Similarly no signals could be detected through the 270 feet of core masonry from Belzoni's chamber to the North face of the pyramid. Tests were then made at the Great Pyramid with the same negative results. Thus both pyramids were shown conclusively to have high radio-frequency losses.

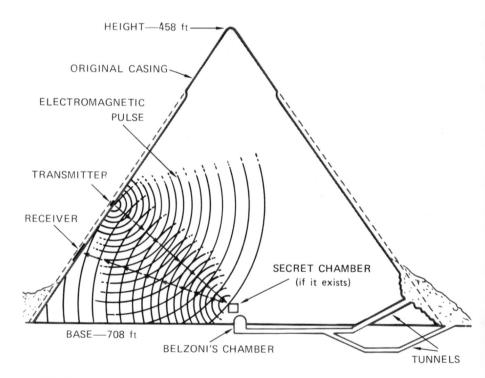

HEIGHT—458 ft

ORIGINAL CASING

ELECTROMAGNETIC PULSE

TRANSMITTER

RECEIVER

SECRET CHAMBER
(if it exists)

BASE—708 ft

BELZONI'S CHAMBER

TUNNELS

ELECTROMAGNETIC PROBING OF EGYPTIAN PYRAMIDS

Stanford Research Institute

The immediate question was, of course, why are the energy losses so high when tests made in the United States were successful for even greater distances. Although it was known that high moisture content in soil and rock produces high radio-frequency losses, the general knowledge that the climate of Egypt is dry (rainfall at Giza less than 1 inch per year) had ruled out any problems due to moisture. However, tests showed that this indeed was the root of the problem. In spite of the low annual rainfall and the warm climate, the average humidity level inside the pyramids was found to be 83 per cent.

The reason given by the experimenters, for the high humidity, is the prevailing North wind at Giza, bringing with it the damp marine air from the Mediterranean Sea. It was also noted that the limestone bedrock and core masonry of the pyramids is quite porous (as far as rocks go) and there is a movement of water vapour from the ground water table, below the ground surface, up through the pyramids to the atmosphere, thus providing a high humidity in the structures.

It has been calculated that within the masonry of Chephren's pyramid, the total quantity of water and water vapour amounts to 100 million gallons. With this amount of moisture, the experiments have proved that this particular method of exploration using radio waves is, unfortunately, not suitable for testing the Giza Pyramids.

Under the name of "Psycho-phenomenon," investigations are currently in progress that are experimenting with models of the Great Pyramid to determine possible physical, chemical and biological process that may be going on inside that shape. Perhaps there exists an accumulation of electromagnetic waves, cosmic rays or some unknown "energy".

Some of the claims of what pyramid energy can do include: preservation of food, purification of water, razor blade sharpening, enhancement of meditation, shortening of healing time, increased concentration, improving personal relationships and effecting plant growth. One of the earliest investigators of pyramid energy, the late Verne L. Cameron of California, U.S.A., in 1953 noted the effect of cones and pyramids in stimulating plant growth.

Although no acceptable scientific evidence exists that proves the pyramid form is a generator of what is called "pyramid energy", there are many indications that the geometric form of a pyramid may have the ability to generate a "soft energy" which can energize or preserve life. It is speculated that the pyramid form traps some form of universal energy that is attracted by the Earth's gravitational pull, converting it into a concentrated and useable "soft energy".

Ian Woods B.L.A. (pyramid design researcher) of Toronto, Canada, theorizes pyramid energy is an "energy which affects life by encouraging the cells in animal, vegetable and mineral matter to resonate at a special frequency. In other words, the vibration of the pyramid causes the cells to match vibration with itself. This action has the ability to return organisms back to their 'natural vibration' and in so doing, energizes the cells of living organisms or preserves the cells of non-living organisms. Under the influence of pyramid energy then, an organism can realize a greater potential." (Pyramid Design - 1976)

The above theory is based on the hypothesis that all forms resonate energy and that a pyramid is a special form in that it resonates with a certain form of energy that can be beneficial for mankind. If this be true then perhaps the greatest potential of pyramid forms (energy?) will be found in the research being done with Pyramid Greenhouses. Current experimenters are reporting that the pyramid effect is causing plants to grow more quickly and vigorously and certain food plants to yield an increase of three times more than usual.

Experiments dealing with the reaction of solar energy in relationship to forms is currently being conducted by one research architect (Ralph L. Knowles) who recently performed a remarkable analysis of the solar energy flowing into Pueblos as a demonstration of what might be expected if such factors were considered in the design of buildings. He suggests that if the energy flows of an entire area were known, then it would be possible to design structures and urban layouts that would take advantage of them.

While such scientific investigations are being conducted, theories propounded by pseudo-scientific, science-fiction and sensational authors are constantly being published which do nothing more than hinder legitimate research.

WHO WAS THE BUILDER?

To ascribe to a certain personage the actual building or superintending of the building of the Pyramid of Giza has been the object of much research. No archaeological or historical evidence has been found to positively identify the builder. There is a tradition that has existed since ancient times; that the builder was Almodad, the eldest of the thirteen sons of Joktan (Genesis 10:26). Almodad, whose name means "God is a friend", is described in the Chaldaic Paraphrase of Jonathan, as the Inventor of Geometry and the Measurer of the Earth. Certainly the Great Pyramid was constructed according to a marvelous geometric design.

Peleg, the uncle of Almodad (Genesis 10:25-26) and the son of Eber or Heber whose descendants became known as Hebrews, was also contemporary with the period of the building of the Great Pyramid. We read of Peleg: "in his days was the earth divided," (Genesis 10:25; I Chronicles 1:19).

Since the earth is incapable of separation from something else we must conceive some division of the earth which would not destroy its unity. A division effected geometrically, such as into degrees, minutes and seconds would be applicable to the expression, "was divided." The location of the Great Pyramid, which divides the land surfaces of the world into equal parts — all the land east of the meridian on which the Pyramid stands being equal (within the limits of computation) to that west of it, is physical application of that expression.

Almodad and his family came from the area of Arabia (Genesis: 10:30). This is consistent with the records of ancient historians revealing Arabia as the eastern territory from which the builders of the Pyramid came.

Job, the youngest brother of Almodad, has also been mentioned in connection with the building of the Great Pyramid. In the 38th chapter of the Book of Job the Almighty speaks to Job as if he were the identical person who had laid the measures of the Pyramid, stretched the lines upon it, set its foundations in their sockets, and laid the corner stone.

It appears the object of the passage is to convince Job of his incompetency to judge and understand God. The address seems to sound as if the Creator intended to say to him, "You laid the foundations of the great structure in Egypt, but where were you when I laid the foundations of the far greater pyramid of the earth? You laid the measures on the pyramid in Egypt, but who laid the measures of the earth, and streched the line upon it? You fastened down in sockets the foundation of the pyramid in Egypt, but whereupon are the foundations of the earth fastened? You laid the corner stone amid songs and jubilations, but who laid the cornerstone of the earth when the celestial morning stars sang together, and all the heavenly sons of God shouted for joy?"

The image is unquestionably that of the Great Pyramid and is suggestive that it was the builder of that pyramid who is thus addressed.

Another personage whose name is often linked with the building of the Pyramid is Enoch, who lived 365 years (Gen. 5:23) and perhaps to be more exact (since there are 365.242 days in a year) 365.242 years, the value of the solar year. The Great Pyramid has been referred to, by ancient historians, as the "Pillar of Enoch". Bible Chronologists, however, have established that Enoch was no longer living on the earth, at the time of the building of the Pyramid.

Josephus, the 1st century A.D. historian, referring to the descendants of Seth wrote: "They were the inventors of the peculiar sort of wisdom which is concerned with the heavenly bodies and their order. And that their inventions might not be lost before they were sufficiently known...they made two pillars; the one of brick, the other of stone; they inscribed their discoveries on them both..."

Josephus goes on to state that the pillar of stone "remains in the land of Siriad to this day" (A.D. 37-95). Siriad would indicate the Siriadic, or Sirius worshipping land of Egypt, where Sirius was venerated as the star of Isis.

The identity of the builder of the Great Pyramid remains one of its hidden secrets. We may conclude, however, from the available evidence we have that a descendant of Shem, a Shemite, was its builder. It is noted that they were descendants of Enoch to whom God has given revelations concerning the "times and cycles of the heavenly luminaries" and from Noah who had received special revelations in the sciences of measures, mechanics, and all the superior wisdom embodied in the Great Pyramid.

WHO WAS THE ARCHITECT?

The Great Pyramid, which has stood at the border of the great Sahara Desert as a silent witness for more than 4,000 years, now speaks in modern scientific terms. Erected at a time when humanity had more crude ideas of this universe and even of our own earth, this "witness" could not be understood before this present scientific age.

The perfect accuracy of all the various geodetic and astronomical statistics which man was unable to ascertain until modern times, after the development of trigonometrical knowledge and the invention of modern appliances, is evidence of Divine Revelation. Regardless of who is found to have supervised its construction, the Architect of the Great Pyramid stands revealed as none other than Almighty God, the Creator of the Universe.

Notwithstanding the fact that no nation of antiquity on earth possessed the knowledge revealed by the design of the Great Pyramid or understood it, some may reject its Divine Inspiration.

God, seemingly, anticipated man's need for additional evidential value of the Pyramid's Divine testimony and gave a line of proof which connot be anticipated or counterfeited. God appointed the test, which we are to apply, in Isaiah 46: 9-10: *"I am God, and there is none like Me, declaring the end from the beginning."* If it can be shown that the design of the Great Pyramid embodies a prophetic chronology, then we have the very evidence which God Himself has declared shall be proof that the design is from Him.

A suggestion for looking for this prophetic message in the Great Pyramid was revealed in the translation of an ancient Arabic writing, the Akbar Ezzeman M.S., which states that the Great Pyramid contains "the wisdom and acquirements in the different arts and sciences...the sciences of arithmetic and geometry, that they might remain as records for the benefit of those who could afterwards comprehend them...the positions of the stars and their cycles; together with the history and chronicle of the time past (and) of that which is to come."

The factual evidence that the Great Pyramid contains a prophetic chronology can be demonstrated from the actual passage lengths, lengths being proportionate to the respective ages which they represent.

This remarkable discovery was made possible by a study of the geometric circle upon which the Great Pyramid is designed, the year circle, sometimes referred to as the "Enoch Circle". This circle, found by drawing a circle whose diameter equals the length of the Ante-Chamber in the Pyramid was discovered to have a circumference of 365.242 Pyramid inches.

Not only was this the exact number of days of our solar year, it was also the number of years expressed in decimals, that Enoch lived on earth, that is, 365 years, 88 days, 9 hours.* Thus, inches may be expressed in terms of years.

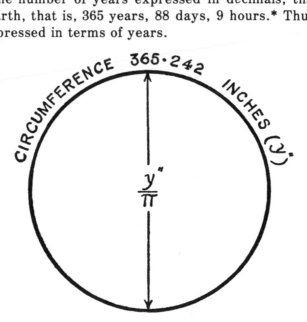

THE YEAR CIRCLE
(Enoch Circle)

The origin of the scale of the Biblical chronological prophecy, 1 day = 1 year, and that of the Great Pyramid's chronograph, 1 inch = 1 year, can thus both be traced back to the Enoch Circle, as can the Sacred Cubit itself.

So much of the Great Pyramid's chronological prophecy has now been realized in history that the scale 1 inch = 1 year has been incontrovertably proven.

---

* The original prophetic writings of Enoch must not be confused with the versions of the apocyrphal "Book of Enoch" compiled 4,000 years later, about the 2nd century B.C.

PROOF OF DIVINE AUTHORSHIP

In establishing a prophetic chronology it is necessary to have a starting point. Several unique factors determine this starting point.

First, the Descending Passage, starting from the outside north slope of the Pyramid, has at a distance of about 40 feet from the entrance, straight knife-edge lines cut from roof to floor, one on each side and exactly opposite each other. Their appearance on the otherwise perfectly smooth walls of the passage certainly suggests that they are intended as a clear zero line or datum line from which to take measurements. They are called the "Scored Lines."

Second, the Descending Passage is found to be in exact alignment with the true north. In response to a question if the North Star ever shone directly down the Descending Passage, Sir John Herschel, the famous Astronomer Royal of England, ascertained in 1840 that only in the 22nd century B.C. did the then North Star or Pole Star, known as Draconis (Dragon Star), so shine. No other Pole Star in history has ever been in that exact position.

Sir John also found that at the very same time, the beautiful and much admired little stellar cluster, the Pleiades or "Seven Sisters," in the constellation of Taurus (the Bull), was in alignment with the Scored Lines. (The Pleiades or Seven Stars are referred to in the Book of Job (38:31) *"Canst thou bind the sweet influences of Pleiades. or loose the bands of Orion?"* Also in Amos (5:8) *"Seek him that maketh the seven Stars and Orion."* Alcyone, the principal star of the cluster is classified as *Tarui* by astronomers.)

The date at which the Dragon Star and the Pleiades were in those precise positions relative to the Pyramid was the vernal equinox of the year 2141 B.C. This particular year is singled out, by the Pyramid, as the year of reference in respect to chronological measurements. Thus the Pyramid's entire prophetic chronograph is astronomically fixed.

Measurements in inches, backward or forward from the Scored Lines, represent the corresponding number of years before or after that astronomically fixed date. To test the accuracy of this starting date was relatively simple. The date, being so far back in history, allows ample testing against known recorded historical events. Putting it to the actual test consisted of measuring the passages and chambers up and down from the Scored Lines, counting one year for each inch.

The Pyramid is not made of elastic, but of rigid stone, so the measurements cannot be stretched nor shortened. We can only take the dimensions of the passages, just as they were constructed by the ancient builders, and let the results take care of themselves.

The distance measuring back up the Descending Passage from the Scored Lines is 482 Pyramid inches, representing 482 years. Counting 482 years back from the datum line of 2141 B.C. brings us to the year 2623 B.C. This was the year that work on the construction of the Great Pyramid began. (See dia. pg. 77).

As the passages of the Pyramid's interior symbolized ages which were then future, this date for the entrance to the Pyramid was most appropriate.

Measuring 688 inches beyond the Scored Lines down the Descending Passage to an aperture appearing in the roof, marks the entrance to the Ascending Passage. Progressing 688 years from 2141 B.C. gives the date of 1453 B.C. This was the date of the Exodus of the Israelites from Egypt and their receiving the Divine Law, through Moses, on Mt. Sinai.

The institution of the Passover (the first feature of the Law) marked the beginning of the age commonly referred to as the "Dispensation of the Law" (Mosaic Law), a period of time from the Exodus and giving of the Law to man as a way to eternal life and ending at the Crucifixion of Jesus Christ. Being the first man able to keep the Law inviolate, He fulfilled it, thus ending that dispensation.

This period of time has been considered, by most Bible chronologists, as being 1485 years. As the date for the Exodus was 1453 B.C. and that for the Crucifixion was A.D. 33, the interval between them is inflexible 1485 years.

Measuring up the Ascending Passage at the given scale of an inch to a year, we find the length is 1485 inches and therefore the end of the passage marks precisely the date A.D. 33 (Spring). (For the sake of any who may not be used to chronological reckoning, the rule for ascertaining the A.D. date required is to deduct the figures of the B.C. date from the total period and add 1, thus 1485 − 1453 + 1 = A.D. 33).

This period of time, being rigidly fixed as 1485 years so far as the Pyramid evidence is concerned, clearly shows that the Ascending Passage represents the Law Dispensation period.

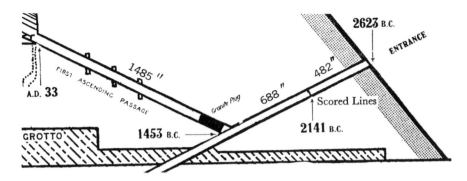

Between a point where the floor level of the Queen's Chamber intersects with the floor of the Ascending Passage and the upper end of the Ascending Passage, a geometric triangle is formed. The north end of its base marks the date September 29, 2 B.C. and the apex marks the date April 3, A.D. 33.

Archaeological findings have recently established September 29, 2 B.C. as the birth of Christ and April 3, A.D. 33 as the precise day of His Crucifixion. The base length of 30.043 Pyramid inches converted to years and projected on the slope of the Ascending Passage marks October 14, A.D. 29 which is the date of His baptism, exactly 3½ years before His death on Calvary.

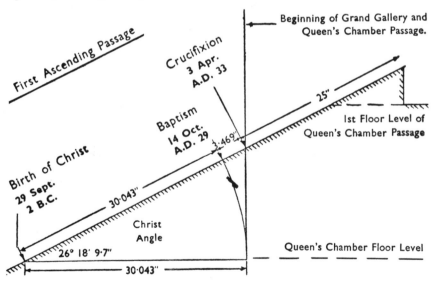

CHRIST TRIANGLE

The amazing and conclusive result of applying the inch-years scale produced the PROOF OF DIVINE REVELATION. Erected over 2600 years before the Crucifixion of Christ and even 1000 years before the first books of the Bible were written, the Great Pyramid is found to contain in its design a prophetic chronology, recorded centuries before the actual events took place and also long before any of the Biblical prophecies, concerning Christ were uttered.

Although erected at a time when humanity had most crude ideas of the universe and even of our own Earth, the Pyramid built under the Divine inspiration, displays the Christian religion upon a scientific basis. Modern discovery and research have revealed the fact that this, the world's most massive edifice, symbolically and by measurement, proclaim Jesus Christ as the Redeemer of Israel and the Savior of the World. His birth, His baptismal, His Life, His death, His resurrection and ascension—is the central theme of the Great Pyramid as well as of the Bible.

Continuing proof of prophetic chronology is found by measuring the lofty passage following after and at the same slope as the Ascending Passage. This passage, known as the Grand Gallery, would represent the age from Jesus' day onward. In this age, represented thereby, the "Gospel of the Kingdom" has also "been preached in all the world, for a witness unto all nations".

On applying the chronological test to the Grand Gallery, as we did to the previous passages, we again obtain an amazing result. We find its length to be 1881⅓ inches. So, continuing consistently at the rate of an inch to a year, we ascertain that the end of it therefore marks the late summer of A.D. 1914. This date was the ending of the "Seven Times" period of Daniel's prophecy in the Bible (A "time" being 360 years × 7 = 2520 years). The fall of Assyria in 607 B.C. is the starting time and termination is the beginning of "the time of trouble" with which this age, and indeed this whole world order, is due to be replaced with the inauguration of the New Order. Both Bible time-prophecy and the Great Pyramid's chronograph show the "Times of the Gentiles" were due to run out in 1914.

In the New Testament Our Lord prophesied about the "Times" in Luke 21:24, which reads: *"Jerusalem shall be trodden down of the Gentiles, until the times of the Gentiles be fulfilled."* In accordance with this prophecy, Jerusalem has been oppressed by one heathen power after another, all down the centuries, from the first century of the Christian era. In 1914 the last oppressor, Turkey, was challenged by Britain, and the ensuing World War I found Jerusalem delivered from the hands of its last oppressor.

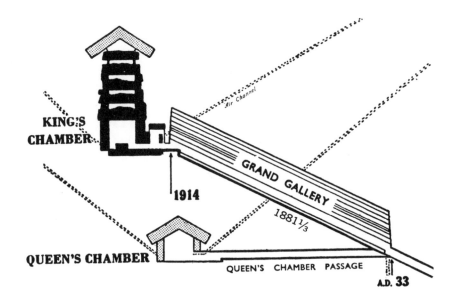

It is interesting to note that the delivery of Jerusalem, in December of 1917 by General Allenby of the British Army, was also precisely a prophetic "Seven times" (2,520 years) after 604 B.C., the date when Nebuchadnezzar first came against Jerusalem and took the city and led away that segment of the tribe of Judah captive into Babylon. Even the manner in which the city was delivered in 1917 was explicitly foretold by the Prophet Isaiah (Isaiah 31:5): *"As birds flying, so will the Lord of Hosts defend Jerusalem; defending, also He will deliver it; and passing over, He will preserve it."*

British airplanes flew low at high speed, to and fro over the city, and scared the Turks into surrender without firing a shot, and at the same time defended the city against Turkish planes. In detailed fulfillment of Isaiah, the number 14 Bomber Squadron of the Royal Flying Corps (the old name for what is now the R.A.F.) took Jerusalem "as flying birds" and defended it, and passing over it, preserved it. An indication of the Divine planning, in every detail, may be found in the motto, inscribed on the badge of the bomber squadron chosen for the task, which read: "I spread my wings and keep my promise."

The verdict of time, again gives confirmation of the truth of the inch-year scale of chronological prophecy, built into the design of the Great Pyramid, and added validity to the argument for its Divine Authorship.

The Incomparable Christ

JESUS, THE CHRIST, born of a virgin nearly 2,000 years ago, lived in poverty and was reared in obscurity. He did not travel extensively.

He possessed neither wealth nor high social standing. His relatives were inconspicuous, and had neither training nor formal education.

In infancy He startled a king; in childhood He puzzled doctors; in manhood He ruled the course of nature, walked upon the billows as if pavements, and hushed the sea to sleep.

He healed the multitudes without medicine and made no charge for His service.

He never wrote a book, and yet many times more books have been written about Him than about anyone else who has ever lived. His discourses and teaching have been translated into over 1,000 languages and have a circulation many times greater than that of any other writings in existence.

He never wrote a song, and yet He has furnished the theme for more songs than all the songwriters combined.

He never founded a college, but all the schools put together cannot boast of having as many students.

He never marshalled an army, nor drafted a soldier, nor fired a gun; and yet no leader ever had more volunteers who have, under His orders, made more rebels stack arms and surrender without a shot fired.

He never practiced psychiatry, and yet He has healed more broken hearts than all the doctors far and near.

Once each week the wheels of commerce cease their turning and multitudes wend their way to worshipping assemblies to pay homage and respect to Him.

The names of the past proud statesmen of Greece and Rome have come and gone. The names of the past scientists, philosophers, and theologians have come and gone; but the name of this Man abounds more and more. Though time has spread almost 2,000 years between the people of this generation and the scene of His crucifixion, yet He still lives. Herod could not destroy Him, and the grave could not hold Him. God raised Him from the dead.

He stands forth upon the highest pinnacle of heavenly glory, proclaimed of God, acknowledged by angels, adored by saints, and feared by devils, as the living, personal Christ, our Lord and Saviour.

(Most of the above paragraphs are from a tract of the American Tract Society)

THE CHRIST ANGLE

The Great Pyramid's chronological representation depends upon the angle of the slope of the Passage System. This angle (26° 18' 9.7") is called the "Christ Angle" and forms the "Christ Triangle" (page 77).

This angle of slope, when taken as a "rhumb line" (not a great circle arc) bearing north of true east, describes, from the Great Pyramid, a direct route that passes successively over Israel's crossing of the Red Sea (Sea of Reeds), through Bethlehem, and over Israel's crossing of the Jordan. The two crossings define the beginning and ending of the children of Israel's "wanderings," after coming out of Egypt.

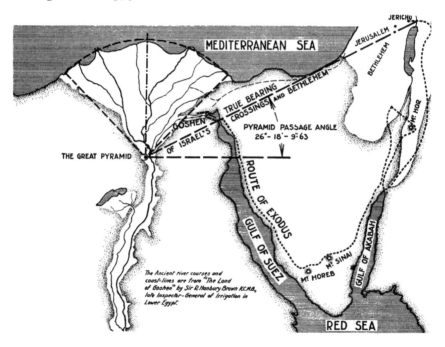

The distance from the Great Pyramid to Bethlehem, along the great circle arc, is 2139 Pyramid furlongs (1 Pyramid furlong = 8000 Pyramid inches). If we start from the Pyramids astronomically fixed datum year 2141 B.C. and apply the scale of a furlong to a year, we obtain not only the place where Jesus was born, Bethlehem, but also the exact time when He was born, considering 2139 years after 2141 B.C. marks the date, 2 B.C.

CHRIST, THE MESSIAH

A confirmation of the chronology of the "Christ Triangle" can be found in the Book of Daniel which not only solves the problem of the "70th week of Daniel" (past or future) but identifies the true Messiah.

In the Book of Daniel, written over 500 years before Jesus came to Earth, it was foretold in Chap.9: 24-27: —

24. *"Seventy weeks are determined upon thy people and upon thy holy city, to finish the transgression, and to make an end of sins, and to make reconciliation for iniquity, and to bring in everlasting righteousness, and to seal up the vision and prophecy, and to annoint the most HOLY."*

25. *"Know therefore and understand, that from the going forth of the commandment to restore and to build Jerusalem unto the Messiah the Prince shall be seven weeks, and threescore and two weeks: the street shall be built again, and the wall, even in troublous times."*

26. *"And after threescore and two weeks shall Messiah be cut off, but not for Himself: and the people of the prince that shall come shall destroy the city and the sanctuary; and the end thereof shall be with a flood, and unto the end of the war desolations are determined."*

27. *"And he shall confirm the covenant with many for one week: and in the midst of the week he shall cause the sacrifice and the oblation to cease, and for the overspreading of abominations he shall make it desolate, even until the consummation, and that determined shall be poured upon the desolate."*

All of the above enumerated events, given in the prophecy, were due to be accomplished by the close of the 70 "weeks." God has His own scale for chronological prophecies and this is stated in Ezekiel 4:6, *"I have appointed thee each day for a year."* The scale is 1 day to a year. This scale if applicable throughout the Bible. Seventy weeks would be (70 x 7) 490 prophetic days, equaling 490 years. The following tabulation shows these prophecies and their fulfillments.

The Prophecy	The Fulfillment
(Daniel, chapter 9, verse 24)	*(New Testament)*

"To finish the transgression and to make an end of sins."	*"Behold the Lamb of God (Christ) which taketh away the sin of the world" (John 1:29).*
	Christ died for our sins" (I Cor. 15:3). "Jesus Christ . . . this man, after he had offered one sacrifice for sins for ever, sat down on the right hand of God" (Hebrews 10:10-12).
"To make reconciliation for iniquity and to bring in everlasting righteousness."	*"Christ died for the ungodly . . . When we were enemies we were reconciled to God by the death of His Son" (Romans 5:6, 10).*
	"If any man sin we have an advocate with the Father, Jesus Christ the righteous, and he is the propitiation for our sins: and not for ours only, but also for the sins of the whole world" (I John 2:1-2).
	"For God so loved the world that He gave His only begotten Son, that whosoever believeth in Him should not perish, but have everlasting life" (John 3:16).
"To seal up the vision and the prophecy"	*The vision and the prophecy was fulfilled in Jesus Christ (the Messiah) as recorded in the New Testament. Furthermore Jesus Christ, Himself, quoted Daniel's prophecies, thus confirming Daniel as a Prophet.*
"To anoint the most Holy."	*Christ Himself chose 12 Apostles, who were appointed to form the foundation of the coming Heavenly Kingdom (Rev. 21:14). These, as the most holy, were anointed by the Holy Spirit, at Pentecost, the 50th day after Christ's resurrection and given miraculous powers.*

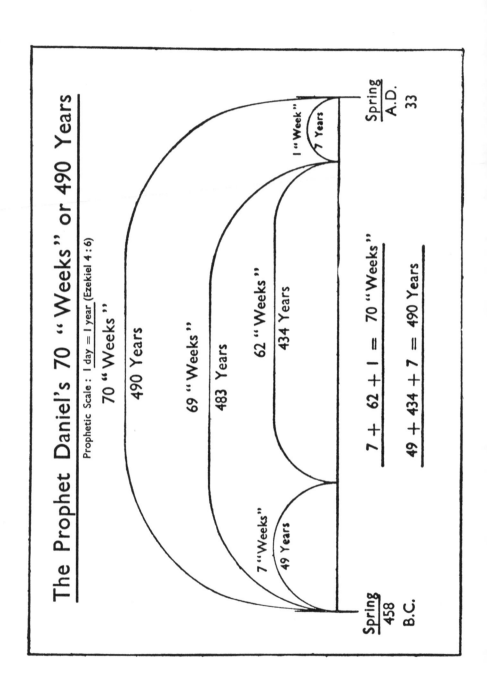

The Prophet Daniel's 70 "Weeks" or 490 Years

Prophetic Scale : 1 day = 1 year (Ezekiel 4 : 6)

70 "Weeks"

490 Years

69 "Weeks"

483 Years

62 "Weeks"

434 Years

7 "Weeks"

49 Years

1 "Week"

7 Years

Spring
458
B.C.

Spring
A.D.
33

7 + 62 + 1 = 70 "Weeks"

49 + 434 + 7 = 490 Years

To find the time of Christ's death and resurrection, as foretold in Daniel's prophecy, we must therefore ascertain the beginning of the 70 "weeks" and count 490 years from that date. Verse 25 gives the beginning as the "going forth of the commandment to restore and to build Jerusalem," which would be the SECOND return of the Israelites from Babylonian Captivity. The first was in the days of Cyrus, when some returned to rebuild the Temple; the second, in the days of Ezra and Nehemiah, when another contingent returned to restore the city and the walls.

Thus, Ezra received the commandment to set out for Jerusalem in the month of Nisan, of Artaxerxes' 7th year (hence Nisan 458 B.C.). He arrived, in Jerusalem, four months later. Whether we count by the imperial and general Nisan-to-Nisan accession year reckoning Artaxerxes' reign or by the unusual Tishri-to-Tishri, non-accession year system (adopted in the Book of Nehemiah) Nisan of Artaxerxes' 7th year is, by both systems, the Nisan of 458 B.C.

Now, clearly 70 prophetic "weeks" (490 years) after Nisan 458 B.C. brings us to Nisan, A.D. 33 (490 - 458 $+$ 1 $=$ 33), the month and year of Christ's death and resurrection, as indicated in the Great Pyramid.

One more important matter should be considered. In verse 27 we are informed that in the middle of the 70th "week," sacrifice and oblation would cease. Christ offered Himself for sacrifice and was accepted (His baptism) half a "week" (3½ years) before the end of Daniel's 70 "weeks," or, in other words, at the end of 69½ prophetic "weeks" or 486½ actual years (586½ - 457¾ $=$ 28¾ A.D. $=$ Autumn A.D. 29).

Thus in the midst of the 70th "week," He (Christ) caused sacrifice and oblation to cease, precisely as foretold five centuries before. this, too, is in full harmony with the statement in verse 26 that after the 7 weeks and 62 weeks, or after the 69 weeks, (during the 70th week), *Messiah*, would be "cut off, but not for himself."

The sacrifice of Jesus, the *Messiah*, began when He was 30 years old and was completely consummated when He was 33½ years old, thereby ending the 70th week of Daniel. All this, revealed in the Christ Triangle, shows Bible Chronology and Pyramid Chronology to be harmonious.

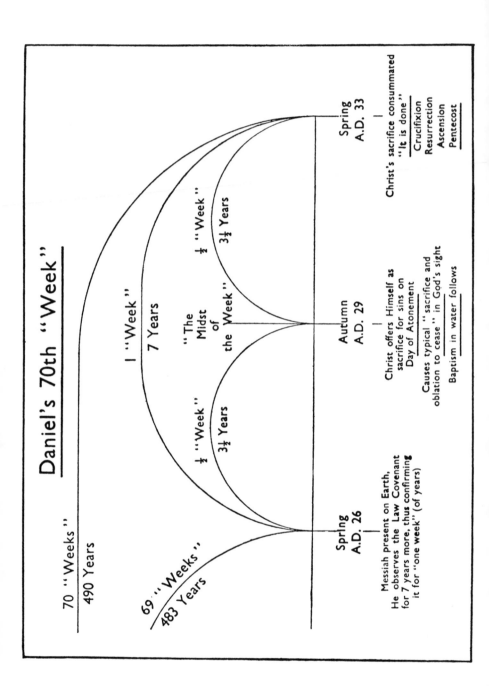

Daniel's 70th "Week"

70 "Weeks"

490 Years

69 "Weeks"

483 Years

1 "Week"

7 Years

½ "Week"

3½ Years

"The Midst of the Week"

½ "Week"

3½ Years

Spring A.D. 26

Messiah present on Earth, He observes the Law Covenant for 7 years more, thus confirming it for "one week" (of years)

Autumn A.D. 29

Christ offers Himself as sacrifice for sins on Day of Atonement

Causes typical "sacrifice and oblation to cease" in God's sight

Baptism in water follows

Spring A.D. 33

Christ's sacrifice consummated "It is done"

Crucifixion
Resurrection
Ascension
Pentecost

DISPLACEMENT FACTOR

Diodorus, who saw the Great Pyramid in its original state, tells us that it never had a "top-stone." Bible scholars know it as "the stone which the builders rejected." (Matt. 21:42) Modern investigations have revealed the reason the Pyramid was left unfinished. In the course of measuring the Pyramid, several occurrences of the number 286.1 P. inches were noted. Today, it is known as the "Displacement Factor."

The passage entering the Great Pyramid was east of the Pyramid's north-south axis by 286.1 P. inches. The height of the Grand Gallery exceeds that of the First Ascending Passage by that same figure. The perimeter of the top platform made to receive the Cap-stone is too short by that same measurement. In light of the amazing scientific knowledge displayed in the design and construction of the Great Pyramid, one might wonder how such a significant error could occur.

The answer is found in the Ante-Chamber known as the "drawing office" of the Pyramid. Its geometric design supplies us with all the important dimensions of the Pyramid on the scale of 1:100. According to the Ante-Chamber's geometry, the side of the base is 36,524 P. inches, the number of days in a century. The length of the Ante-Chamber, 116.2603 P. inches, is equal to the diameter of a circle whose circumference is 365.24235 P. inches – one of five examples found in the Ante-Chamber. Excavations by the Egyptian Government in 1925 revealed that the base circuit of the Pyramid is 36,238 P. inches, which is exactly 286.1 P. inches short of the Architect's design.

The core masonry was built correctly according to the design, but each side was very slightly hollowed in at the center. Thus, the base was not a perfect square. Had the workers laid the Casing Stones at an even thickness upon the core, there would have been no problem. Then, the base would have measured the required 36,524.2 P. inches in perimeter. However, in tapering the Casing Stones to half the thickness needed, the base was 286.1 P. inches short of the needed design.

In the following plan, much exaggerated in its proportions, the inner line represents the extent of the core masonry; the shaded band, the Casing Stones as laid by the builders; the dotted outer lines, the additional area that should have been covered by the Casing Stones.

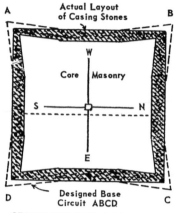

GREAT PYRAMID BASE PLAN
Center line of Passage System 286.1 P. inches E. of central N. to S. line

It appears the Architect's Plan was violated right at the commencement of the building, when the workmen laid the first course of the Casing Stones slightly smaller than the design. Perhaps they reasoned that a straight line would be far more sensible, and also, the difference was so small, only about 2 yards in a length of 250, it would not matter. However, their transgression had immediate and far-reaching results. It meant that from the bottom to the top of the Great Pyramid, the building would be imperfect.

In studying the construction and symbolism of the Great Pyramid it soon becomes apparent that the 286.1 P. inches was an intentional error, symbolizing man's fall or displacement from God's purpose for man. The Cap-Stone, symbolizing Christ, the Chief Corner-Stone and Head Stone of the Corner could not contain any error or imperfection, hence the builders rejected it. (*The stone which the builders refused is become the head stone of the corner.* Ps. 118:22 and *Unto you therefore which believe he is precious: but unto them which be disobedient, the stone which the builders disallowed, the same is made the head of the corner.* I Peter 2:7)

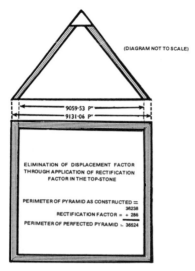

(DIAGRAM NOT TO SCALE)

9059·53 P"

9131·06 P"

ELIMINATION OF DISPLACEMENT FACTOR
THROUGH APPLICATION OF RECTIFICATION
FACTOR IN THE TOP-STONE

PERIMETER OF PYRAMID AS CONSTRUCTED = 36238

RECTIFICATION FACTOR = + 286

PERIMETER OF PERFECTED PYRAMID = 36524

"TOP-STONE" PLACED
AND RESULTANT PERFECTION OF THE GREAT PYRAMID

Only if the sides of the Pyramid were filled out to join with the designed Cap-Stone would the base of the Pyramid be perfect, 36,523 P. inches. Thus the error and imperfection would be rectified, symbolizing the rectification of error and imperfection in mankind by Christ.

THE GREAT PYRAMID

When God of old devised this Plan,
As witness and a guide to man,
He based His symbols and His signs
On truly scientific lines;
For well He knew that in the end,
Would science and religion blend.

Thus for our benefit is shewn,
The Bible symbolized in stone.
And if God's Holy Book you love,
And wish Jehovah's Words to prove,
His myst'ries can be seen, long hid,
In The Divine Great Pyramid.

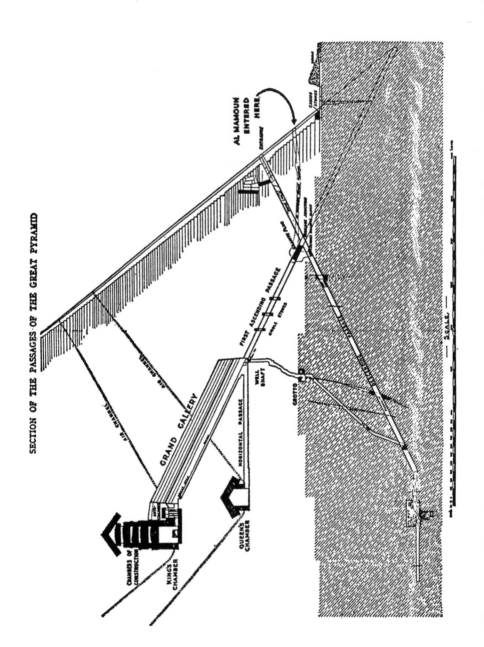

SECTION OF THE PASSAGES OF THE GREAT PYRAMID

WHY WAS IT BUILT?

It is logical to conclude from the evidence presented that the Great Pyramid of Giza was built under Divine Inspiration. This fact in itself proves that God, in His infinite wisdom, thought it necessary for our instruction. It is now up to man to make use of knowledge it contains.

We have the suggestion, in Isaiah 19:20, that the Pyramid is a witness. One might ask, "we have the Bible, does God need another witness?" The answer "yes" would be consistent with the Bible; that the evidence of "two witnesses" shall establish a matter. Also the need for a second witness is shown by the fact that we have had the evidence of the Bible all through the ages, which, for those who can believe it, is God's infallible Word. But, our belief in this fundamental fact has not been very strong. The critic and the modernist have not found it difficult to undermine the faith of the great masses, of our time, in the reliability of the Bible record.

An analysis of the Great Pyramid suggests the following answers to the question; why was it built?

First, to convey new proof to men in the present age, in spite of, and yet by means of, modern science, as to the existence of the personal God of Scripture. We live in a skeptical as well as in a scientific age. In religion and in science mankind embraces rationalism and unfaith. Humanity has become boastful of its intellectual power, and proudly aiming to be "as God," it has become thoroughly materialistic, God seemingly anticipated that this age would lapse into agnosticism and prepared for it. This stone witness was designed to corroborate His Revelation. That the Pyramid was designed for this age is evident by the fact that its revelation did not come to light centuries ago.

Second, to reaffirm the prophecies of the Old Testament Scriptures which reach that of the seed of the woman, without the man, a Divine Saviour and Redeemer was to arise and appear among men. That was an actual historical event and took place at a definite preordained date.

Third, to proclaim Jesus Christ as the Saviour of man. Did you never read in the Scriptures, *"The Stone which the builders rejected, the same is become the head of the corner: this is the Lord's doing, and it is marvelous in our eyes"* (Matthew 21:42). *"Jesus Christ Himself being the chief corner stone; In whom all the*

building fitly framed together unto an holy temple in the Lord: "
(Ephesians 2:20,21). Our Lord Jesus Christ is referred to in these
passages as the "Chief Corner Stone." He is the Stone which the
builders rejected, and is yet to become "the head of the corner,"
that is the head of that pyramid representing His Kingdom here
upon earth, which kingdom is now imminent.

Fourth, to give added evidence of His second coming, when He
shall descend as the Lord from Heaven, with the view of reigning
over all mankind, in one all just, beneficent omnipotent rule. This
reign likewise is shown to be historical and to commence on a
definite prearranged date.

God's Stone Witness, The Great Pyramid designed by the Divine
Architect in the dim past, today stands decoded. Within its
structure lie the architectural drawings of God's great plan for our
planet. Now, at the time appointed, it witnesses and proclaims the
now imminent Divine judgments and the glory to follow.

The Great Pyramid, the first and greatest of the Seven Wonders
of the Ancient world, is still the greatest Wonder of the World.

THE CHIEF CORNER STONE

*"He shall bring forward the Top-Stone amid shouts of 'Grace, grace
unto it.'"*
                                                        —Zechariah 4: 7

*"The stone which the builders rejected, the same is become the head of the
corner. This is the LORD's doing, it is marvellous in our eyes."*

                                        Psalm 118: 22, 23

God's Witness of Stone
— The Great Pyramid —

In a dry weary land; in a wilderness lone;
In a desert of sand, is God's Witness of Stone,
So majestic the whole and so deep its design,
It convinces the soul of a Builder Divine.

Over four thousand years, it has stood in that place,
'Mid the sighs and the tears of the poor fallen race.
With its secret unknown some have gazed at this tower,
While Jehovah alone knew the depth of its power.

Now there's wonderful skill, that is seen all within;
Come! behold, if you will, the dark symbols of sin;
And then trace from "the fall" how the Lord doth atone,
Showing hope that's "for all" in this Bible of Stone.

'Tis a chart for the wise, giving signs for that day,
When mankind will arise and pursue the right way;
They'll read the glad story which before was unknown,
And God will have glory through His Witness of Stone!

(*Anon.*)

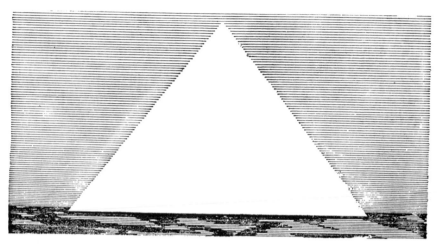

The Glory of The Great Pyramid

Behold this mighty beauteous wonder!
O Pyramid of God's own splendour.
O mighty glorious altar so dear,
Let us hear, let us know of thy secrets made clear.

What a glorious sight to behold;
What marvellous mysteries now unfold.
God's hidden plan revealed to man,
From ages past, at last made known.

Every stone, every inch of thy marvellous being
Are glories, are secrets our hearts are now seeing.
He drew His plan for all mankind
And left it there for us to find.

Thy casing stones of dazzling white
All shining with a heavenly light
Reflect the glories hid within
Reflect the beauty that is Him.

What glories, what secrets, what marvellous truths
Have you held for these many long years.
But now, praise to God, you speak loud and clear
As His Kingdom and glorious Reign nears.

Dixielee Errico.

ACKNOWLEDGEMENT

The object of this booklet has been to provide a simple explanation for beginners in the study of Pyramidology. Limited space dictated the omission of many facts, as well as future prophetic dates. Their revelation is left for the author of more comprehensive works on the subject.

It should be acknowledged that the material contained herein was compiled from the labor and efforts of many authorities on the Great Pyramid, both present and past. No originality is claimed for the technical and mathematical phases.

This treatise, as well as all others written in the century, is indebted to the great pioneers of Pyramidology: John Greaves, Robert Menzies, Professor C. Piazzi Smyth (Astronomer Royal for Scotland), the Egyptologists Col. Howard Vyse and W.M. Flinders Petrie, John and Morton Edgar, and James Rutherford.

A large portion of this material is taken from the current works of the late Dr. Adam Rutherford, F.R.A.S.,F.R.G.S., Pyramidologist. Permission to reprint same is gratefully acknowledged.

E. RAYMOND CAPT

THE ORIGINAL GREAT SEAL

OF THE

UNITED STATES OF AMERICA

REVERSE SIDE

Annuit coeptis = He hath prospered our beginnings

Novus ordo seclorum = A New Order of Ages

"Behold, I lay in Sion a chief corner stone, elect, precious: and he that believes on Him shall not be confounded." —I Peter 2:6.